Complete
Writing Lessons

For

The Middle Grades

By

Marjorie Frank

Illustrated By Kathleen Bullock

Illustrations and cover design by Kathleen Bullock
Edited by Sally D. Sharpe

ISBN 0-86530-160-3

Contents

TABLE OF CONTENTS

THE WRITING LESSONS

Before You Use This Book . . .

For 15 years I've been listening to teachers talk about writing. I've learned that they're hungry for exciting writing activities. They want loads of great motivators that will help students start writing.

However, teachers are just as interested in the entire writing process. In fact, more than anything else, teachers ask for help with the steps that follow the great motivating activity. They want to know:

- how to get their students to gather raw material
- how to get kids through the painful "rough draft" stage
- how to get young writers to organize ideas and give form to the written piece
- how to get kids to criticize and polish their own (and others') writing
- how to work on different kinds of writing skills (which ones to work on and when)
- how to evaluate finished products and what to do with them

I wrote IF YOU'RE TRYING TO TEACH KIDS HOW TO WRITE, YOU'VE GOTTA HAVE THIS BOOK! because I believe that teachers must include both the fun activities that stimulate writing and the "heavier" skills that include organizing, refining, and editing. I still believe that. Now, however, teachers want more than ideas or an outline of the writing process. They want actual lessons -- from start to finish. Ideas are easy to come by, but complete directions for implementing ideas are not as easy to find.

COMPLETE WRITING LESSONS FOR THE MIDDLE GRADES is what teachers have requested. Each lesson begins with a high-interest activity that will motivate writers. Then the lesson shows you, the teacher, how to help students collect and organize ideas, write a rough draft, criticize and revise written material, work on specific writing skills, and share the finished product.

These lessons are just the beginning. Once you've used them, you'll be able to create your own. By choosing a topic that sparks the interest of your students and by following the format used in this book, you can turn a topic into a complete writing experience. By the time you've finished this book, you will have grown as much as your writers!

Marjorie Frank

... How To Use The Lessons

The major premise of this book is this: *students learn the writing process best through teacher-directed writing lessons.*

This doesn't mean that kids shouldn't write on their own. They should be writing in diaries and journals, in learning centers, and on independent projects. However, kids do not learn the writing process effectively unless someone teaches it to them, step by step. Once students know the process, they are able to write on their own more successfully.

This is why the activities in this book have been created as teacher-directed lessons. Each lesson of four pages (with the exception of the first lesson of two pages) contains the following elements:

Pages 1 & 2:

> *Teacher Lesson Plan* pages. These pages explain how to guide writers through each step of the writing process for the specific activity. (This process is explained on pages 6 and 7.)

Pages 3 & 4:

> *Student Pages** and/or *Example Pages**.
>
> In every lesson you will find one page (in some cases, two) designed for students to use as a part of one stage of the process. These pages are not meant to be given out as independent writing assignments, but are to be used as a part of a teacher-directed lesson.
>
> Most lessons contain one page of examples. Use the examples to get an idea of some of the kinds of finished products that might result from the lesson. The examples can also serve as motivators for students. Read the examples aloud to get students excited about a topic and to show them possibilities for writing.

*   You have permission to reproduce any of the student or example pages in quantities sufficient for your students.

5

The Writing Process

Each lesson in this book includes these steps:

Romancing
> This step describes a specific activity, discussion, piece of literature, or situation that will get students excited about a writing form or an idea. (Be sure to spend plenty of time on this stage.) When kids don't want to write or can't think of anything to say, they haven't been "romanced" enough.

Collecting
> This step is an extension of the "romancing" stage. Collecting is the most fun and most creative part of the writing process. Each lesson has questions to ask, directions to give, and suggestions to make which help writers gather phrases, words and thoughts for the "raw material". This step goes by quickly, so collect plenty of ideas. (You don't have to use all of the ideas, but you may choose from the assortment.)

Writing
> This step will give you precise instructions and questions which will direct writers as they choose, organize, and combine "raw material" into a written piece.

Praising
> This is the stage in which good writing techniques are reinforced. The positive "judging" of a written piece should not be omitted. Each lesson plan gives specific suggestions for what you can say to help students see the strengths of their writing. You will teach your writers to search for examples of good writing skills and to compliment one another on them. For example:

> *The phrase "shimmering with silence" set a soft, hushed mood.*

> *You chose wonderful "wet" words for this rain poem such as slush, drizzle, slurp, and soggy.*

> *The opening word "Crash!" really grabbed my interest.*

Polishing

This step in the lesson will tell you what to do, say, and ask to get writers reorganizing, refining, and rewriting their pieces. One or two specific editing skills will be emphasized in each lesson. You can also teach kids to ask questions and make suggestions that are helpful to other writers. For example:

It seems these two sentences say the same thing.

"Pretty" is such an overused word. Why don't you use "lovely" instead?

I think this idea might fit better in the next paragraph.

You gave away the ending too soon. Could you add another sentence to increase the suspense?

Showing Off

You give purpose and dignity to a piece of writing when you provide a way for writers to share what they've written. Each lesson suggests one or more ways to "show off" the students' writing.

NOTE:

Be sure to instruct students to check and correct grammar, spelling, and mechanics at the "polishing" stage of each piece.

Writing Skills Checklist

_____ Substituting stronger words (more colorful, more specific)
_____ Replacing inactive verbs with active ones
_____ Eliminating redundancies
_____ Rearranging words within a sentence
_____ Expanding sentences to include more detail
_____ Adding sentences to give more detail
_____ Rearranging sentences for better clarity
_____ Rearranging sentences for better sequence
_____ Rearranging sentences for a different meaning or sound
_____ Writing strong, "catchy" titles
_____ Changing endings
_____ Creating smashing beginnings
_____ Eliminating repetitive ideas or words
_____ Eliminating unnecessary ideas or words
_____ Eliminating long sentences
_____ Deciding if the written piece accomplishes the purpose
_____ Adding words or phrases that create a certain mood
_____ Varying sentence length and structure
_____ Strengthening and varying transitions
_____ Eliminating overused words, phrases, and clichés
_____ Adding more interesting words
_____ Including words that convince
_____ Adapting the content and form to fit the audience
_____ Rearranging ideas to change outcomes
_____ Adding dialogue
_____ Adding understatement, exaggeration, foreshadowing, or irony
_____ Including figures of speech
_____ Varying rhymes and rhythms
_____ Varying punctuation
_____ Examining pieces for bias
_____ Examining pieces for clarity
_____ Examining pieces for effectiveness
_____ Examining pieces for reader appeal

The Writing Lessons

1. In Pursuit Of Trivia

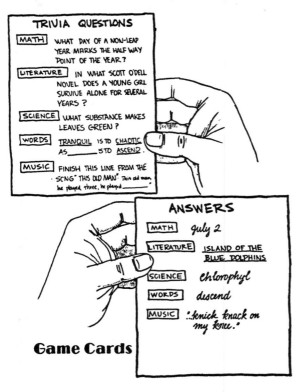

TRIVIA QUESTIONS

MATH — WHAT DAY OF A NON-LEAP YEAR MARKS THE HALF WAY POINT OF THE YEAR?

LITERATURE — IN WHAT SCOTT O'DELL NOVEL DOES A YOUNG GIRL SURVIVE ALONE FOR SEVERAL YEARS?

SCIENCE — WHAT SUBSTANCE MAKES LEAVES GREEN?

WORDS — TRANQUIL IS TO CHAOTIC AS _____ IS TO ASCEND.

MUSIC — FINISH THIS LINE FROM THE SONG "THIS OLD MAN": This old man, he played three, he played _____

ANSWERS

MATH — july 2

LITERATURE — ISLAND OF THE BLUE DOLPHINS

SCIENCE — chlorophyl

WORDS — descend

MUSIC — "knick knack on my knee."

Game Cards

Materials
- trivia game appropriate for students
- textbooks and resource books
- index cards

Romancing
- Have the class play a trivia game. Divide the class into teams of five players each. Each team may consult on each answer.
- After playing, let the students examine several game cards to see how the questions and answers are written. Point out the variety in the kinds of questions and answers.
- Using one textbook (science, for instance), work together to find interesting bits of information. Have the class use the information to write trivia questions.

Collecting
- Agree on five or six categories (use those on page 11 or substitute others). Then let students work in pairs to collect facts from textbooks and other resources. Students should write the facts on scrap paper and label each with the appropriate category.

Writing
- Distribute the student page "A Question Of Trivia" (page 11). Students may use their collected facts to write questions and answers. (You may choose to make changes in the categories.)

Praising
- Each pair trades sheets with another pair of writers. Have the students look for examples which ask questions clearly.
- Point out variety in sentence structure and in the format of questions and answers.

Polishing
- If there are any questions that are too long or confusing, have each pair work to shorten, clarify, or add sufficient information.
- Tell the students to review each question, making sure it is not too obscure or difficult.

Showing Off
- Have each student use index cards to make two trivia cards (questions on one side and answers on the other).
- Have the students put the cards in a box. Now the class has a custom-made trivia game!

A Question Of Trivia

SCIENCE

Question ————————————————
————————————————————————
Answer ————————————————
Question ————————————————
————————————————————————
Answer ————————————————

GEOGRAPHY

Question ————————————————
————————————————————————
Answer ————————————————
Question ————————————————
————————————————————————
Answer ————————————————

MATH

Question ————————————————
————————————————————————
Answer ————————————————
Question ————————————————
————————————————————————
Answer ————————————————

LITERATURE

Question ————————————————
————————————————————————
Answer ————————————————
Question ————————————————
————————————————————————
Answer ————————————————

WORDS

Question ————————————————
————————————————————————
Answer ————————————————
Question ————————————————
————————————————————————
Answer ————————————————

TELEVISION

Question ————————————————
————————————————————————
Answer ————————————————
Question ————————————————
————————————————————————
Answer ————————————————

2. Just Report The Facts

Materials
- ice cream cones (optional)
- markers or crayons

Romancing
- Distribute copies of the student page "The Ice Cream Incident" (page 14), and talk about what is happening in the scenes on the page.
- Have the students read the report that accompanies the picture. Work together to "clean up" the report, making it a truthful account.

    - find and delete incorrect information
    - eliminate opinions and conjectures
    - put events in proper sequence

Collecting
- Hand out copies of the student page "At The Balloon Race" (page 15). Have the students jot down phrases that briefly describe the events shown.

Writing
1) Students may use their collected ideas to make rough outlines of the happenings at the balloon race.
2) Have the students review their outlines to make sure the events are in a logical order.
3) Then, following their outlines, students should begin to write clear, accurate, and objective reports of the contest.

Praising
- Look for phrases and words which give a clear or colorful description of what is happening.
- Point out variety in the sentence structure within the reports.

Polishing
- Have the students rearrange words or sentences to eliminate confusing parts of their reports.
- Warn the students to look for words that suggest personal opinion or exaggeration.

Showing Off
- Students may use markers or crayons to color the scenes. Let the students trade reports with each other to share and compare.

The Ice Cream Incident

 A lot of ice cream was spread all over the sidewalk when a man with a big nose was not watching where he was going. The man had a large stack of cream pies on his bicycle. Mr. McCurdy, a portly man with a moustache, went into the ice cream parlor and ordered an ice cream cone with six dips. He shouldn't have been eating so much ice cream. Just then a news reporter pulled up in front of the parlor. Mr. McCurdy paid for his ice cream and left the store. He was going around the corner to get into his car when the man with the pies ran into him from behind. The pies crashed to the ground. All were ruined.

At The Balloon Race

YOU ARE A WITNESS. WRITE YOUR REPORT HERE.

_____

_____

_____

_____

_____

_____

_____

_____

15

Student Page

3. Guaranteed Cure

Strange Cures:

KNOCK-KNEES :
Only walk sideways

HARD OF HEARING:
hang around folks who talk loudly

SORE THUMB:
stop hammering!

Materials
- collections of American folklore (optional)
- drawing paper, markers, pencils, crayons

Romancing
- Read aloud some "cures" from the example page. (You can find more "cures" in collections of folklore in the library.)
- Let the students share other "cures" or home remedies with which they are familiar.

Collecting
- Work as a group to make the following two lists. (The student page "Absolutely Guaranteed, Money-Back Cure" (page 18) will help you.)
  1) ailments or problems that may bother people
  2) crazy or unusual ideas for cures or solutions

Writing
- Writers may choose to use the collected ideas to write one of the following:
  - a paragraph or two explaining how to cure one ailment
  - several short paragraphs about different cures

Praising
- Comment on unusual, original cures.
- Point out interesting and varied sentence structure.

INSOMNIA:
become a night watchman!

FROG IN THROAT:
place frog on tongue, grab frog as he emerges.

Polishing
- Have the students delete ordinary ideas and replace them with outlandish ones.
- Ask the students the following questions. Have you told the reader what the remedy is? Have you related how to prepare the remedy, how to use it, and when to expect results? Instruct the students to add more details, if necessary.

Showing Off
- Students can use drawing paper and art supplies to illustrate their cures.
- Compile the written pieces and illustrations to make a class medical directory of "sure-fire" remedies.

Absolutely Guaranteed, Money-Back Cure

Here are some examples of ailments or conditions. Try adding more.

headaches	broken heart	indigestion
freckles	measles	indecision
curly hair	old age	hiccups
ingrown toenails	sore throat	jealousy
chicken pox		

_____

_____

_____

Here are some remedies for various ailments.
Add your own ideas.

Spread a mixture of mud on your face.
Wrap a wet sock around your neck.
Stand on your head facing a green wall for
 two hours.
Rub cooked oatmeal on your stomach.
Wear your clothes inside out.
Swallow a live goldfish.
Wash your hair in wallpaper paste.
Walk backward on your knees.

_____

_____

_____

_____

CURE FOR MEASLES:
 DO YOU HAVE THE MEASLES?
GET A LADYBUG TO WALK
ACROSS YOUR FACE AND BODY.
SHE'LL TAKE THE SPOTS WITH
HER. ABSOLUTELY GUARANTEED!

GIGGLE TEE HEE HEE
HEEE HEE HEE
HEE HEE
HEE

SCRATCH!
SCRATCH!

NOW I NEED A CURE FOR
THE TICKLES!

For one or more ailments, write an original cure. You may use the back of this paper.

_____

_____

_____

If your ear is ringing, check to see if the doorbell or phone is ringing. If not, your ears are telling you that someone is talking about you. Stick a finger in your ear. This will cause the gossip to bite his or her tongue.

If you suffer from headaches, here's what you must do. Cover your head with cool yogurt and rest beside a rippling stream. After an hour, wash your head in the stream. If that doesn't help, ask someone to give you a hard kick in the shins. This will make you forget that your head hurts!

If nosebleeds trouble you, one of these remedies is sure to help. Have a gorilla pinch your nose for 10 minutes, or stand on your head and sing "Yankee Doodle". You can also try putting an ice cube on the big toe of your right foot. If none of these remedies work, fry some onions and hold your head over the pan. Sniffing the fumes should cause the blood to harden immediately.

If you want to get rid of acne, this advice will help. Rest 20 minutes each day with wet lettuce leaves on your forehead, or spread cream cheese on your face. You may also wash your face each morning with prune juice. If you still have trouble, glue a chocolate chip to each blemish on your face so that no one will notice the acne!

Examples

4. Blueprint For An Escape

Materials
- crayons and markers

Romancing
- Read aloud "How To Get Bubble Gum Out Of Your Armpit" (page 23).
- Next, read "Quit Monkeying Around" (page 23), and let the students suggest ways that Susan may get out of her predicament. The students may invent serious or outrageously silly solutions.

Collecting
- Brainstorm together to create a list of precarious predicaments.
- Generate a list of words and phrases (see the examples below) that are good for describing confusion, danger, or seemingly unsolvable problems.

peril	impossible	hopeless
no escape	agony	in a pickle
frightfully close	time's running out	exhausted

Writing
1) Have each student choose one of the collected ideas (or a new idea) for a precarious situation.
2) Instruct each student to write a description of a predicament, explaining how the persons involved may remedy the situation.
3) Each student should choose a title for the description which gives the reader an immediate "feel" for the urgency of the situation.

Praising
- Point out interesting, unusual, funny, or surprising phrases and sentences.
- Comment on creative solutions.

Polishing

- Help the students keep their descriptions from being too long by instructing them to eliminate unnecessary information.
- Instruct the students to add words or phrases to make the situations funnier, scarier, more ridiculous, or more surprising.

Showing Off

- Have each student recopy his or her polished description on the student page "Is There A Way Out?" (page 22), and add an illustration in the spot provided.
- Compile the pages to make a volume of "how to escape..." tales. Students can brainstorm to find an appropriate title for the collection of tales.

Is There A Way Out?

_____

_____

_____

_____

_____

_____

_____

_____

How To Get Bubble Gum Out Of Your Armpit

When you fall asleep with gum in your mouth and wake up with gum in your armpit, you've got trouble! This advice might help. Rub ice cubes on the gum, or use an eraser to rub out the gum. Turpentine might help to dissolve the sticky mess! If all else fails, you can always cut out the gum. If you find that solution too extreme, however, just wear a sling and pretend that you have a broken arm!

Quit Monkeying Around

Susan shouldn't have been so close to the cage. All the signs at the zoo warned her not to feed the animals and not to go beyond the railing, but she found the gorillas so fascinating. They pounded rhythmically on their bristled chests, swung from branches, wiggled their backsides at the visitors, and shook all over with excitement when the crowd cheered. The big gorilla, Gonzola, seemed to beckon Susan closer. She was sure he liked her. She never considered that he might be interested in the giant box of caramel corn in her hand.

Susan didn't mean to break the rules. She only wanted to edge a little closer to Gonzola by stepping around the end of the rail. In a flash he had crammed his hand into her caramel corn. When he pulled back, his fingers got stuck in her long hair. Before she could figure out what was happening, Gonzola's hands and her hair were tangled in a mess of soggy caramel corn. As his struggle to be free became wilder, Susan's hair became more tangled.

How can Susan get out of this mess?

Examples

5. But Does It Fly?

Materials
- white typing paper
- scissors, pens, and markers
- assorted books on paper airplane construction (optional)

Romancing
- Give the students plenty of time to make paper airplanes of their own designs. (They may consult books on paper airplanes from the library.)
- Choose a time and place for flying the airplanes.

Collecting
- Distribute copies of the student page "Super Glider" (page 26), and ask the students to follow the directions to make gliders.
- When the gliders have been made and tested, focus again on the directions. Discuss the kinds of instructions that need to be given when telling someone how to make something.
- Have the students unfold their original airplane creations, and ask the students to jot down ideas, phrases, and steps that are important to the construction phase.

YES,
BUT WILL IT
FLY?

Writing

1) Each student should name the airplane he or she has designed.
2) Using the ideas collected, have the students write clear, step-by-step directions for making their original airplanes.

Praising

- Look for directions that are understandable and concise.
- Comment on creative, unique names.

Polishing

- Have the students exchange directions to see if the directions are complete. If students find the directions confusing, they should add details or rearrange steps for better sequence.
- Have the students eliminate unnecessary words.

Showing Off

- Instruct the students to unfold their airplanes and to write polished directions on them.
- Each student can name and decorate his or her plane.
- Let the students fly their planes at the same time. Each student should try to catch one plane.
- Each student then follows the directions written on the plane to make a copy of the plane.

Extra! Extra!

- To extend this activity, have the students create metaphors or phrases about their planes. For example:

  soars through the air like a pop-fly softball
  swift as a rocket
  streaking like a speeding train
  crashing with a crunch

- Have the students write the phrases on their planes. Suspend the planes from the ceiling with string or fishing line.

Super Glider   Directions

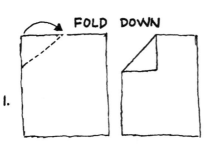
FOLD DOWN

1.

① USE AN 8½" X 11" PAPER. FOLD THE LEFT UPPER CORNER DOWN TO THE MIDDLE.

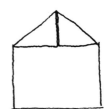

2.

② FOLD THE RIGHT UPPER CORNER DOWN TO THE MIDDLE.

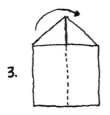

3.

③ FOLD IN HALF.

④ FOLD EACH WING SIDE DOWN TO THE MIDDLE FOLD.

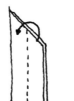

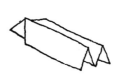

4.

5.

TAPE
TAPE

⑤ TAPE THE FRONT NOSE AND THE BACK EDGE (OPTIONAL).

⑥ HOLD THE PLANE ALONG THE BOTTOM EDGE AND LET IT GLIDE!

Examples

6. Strange Encounters

Materials
- large drawing or cutout of two or three strange creatures (see student pages 30 and 31 for ideas)
- poster board, markers, scissors, glue

Romancing
- Place the "aliens" you've made in front of the room.
- Talk with the class about the places from where the aliens might have come.
- Ask the students to think about what they would say to one of the creatures if they found it in the backyard, under the bed, in a locker at school, etc.

Collecting
- Have the class gather lists of ideas that will help them write conversations they might have with the strange creatures. For example:

  - names of creatures
  - topics to talk about or questions to ask
  - where the creatures' homes might be
  - what the creatures might want to know about humans

Writing
1) Give each student copies of the two student pages "Strange Encounters" (page 30), and "More Strange Encounters" (page 31).
2) For each encounter pictured, the students should write a dialogue inside the balloons.
3) Each student should choose one conversation from each page and write a paragraph below the picture which includes the dialogue, properly punctuated.

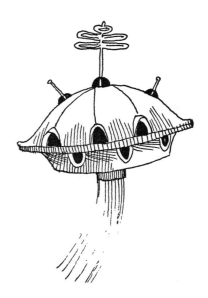

Praising

- Comment on interesting and clever conversations.
- Look for variety in the sentence structure of the dialogue.

Polishing

- Have the students rearrange words and change punctuation, if necessary, until all dialogue is written correctly.
- Students may add more dialogue to their paragraphs in order to make the conversations complete.
- Help them rearrange words and phrases to make the sentences interesting and different. Make sure every sentence does not begin or end with "he said" or "she said".

Showing Off

- The class may use poster board and other art supplies to create strange creatures.
- Students may use their crafted creatures to develop short dramas based on their written conversations, or they may use the creatures to make a bulletin board display showing their strange encounters (with written dialogue).

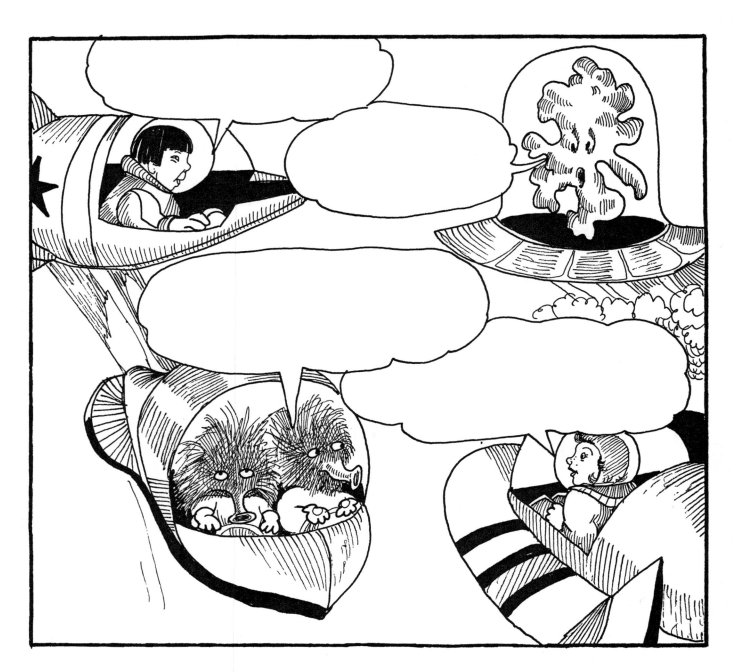

Strange Encounters

_____

_____

_____

_____

_____

_____

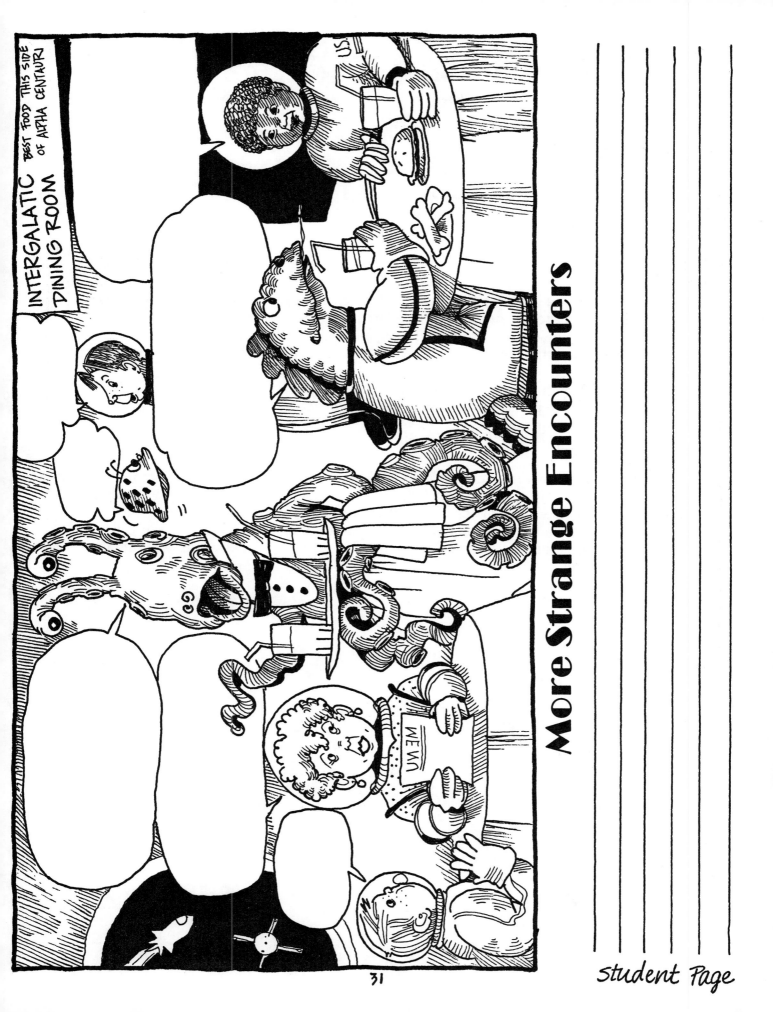

More Strange Encounters

Student Page

7. What A Character!

Materials
- drawing paper and fine-point markers
- scissors and glue

Romancing
- Give each student a copy of the student page "A Case Of Mistaken Identity" (page 34).
- Give the students plenty of time to choose the face parts, to draw the faces of the suspects, and to add an original face and description.
- Let the students share and compare their finished faces.
- Provide the class with paper so that the students may make up their own Ident-I-Kits.
- When the students finish making their Ident-I-Kits, they should each choose one face part from each column to use in creating a character on large drawing paper.

Collecting
- Guide the students through each step on the student page "What's In A Face?" (page 35), and help them gather raw material for a character description (of the character they've just drawn).
- As they write character descriptions on individual papers, make a list of characteristics on the chalkboard. This will help the students generate their own ideas.

OFFICER! I'VE HAD MY POCKET PICKED!

CAN YOU DESCRIBE THIS CHARACTER TO ME, LADDIE?

Writing

1) Guide the students in choosing ideas (from the numbered categories on page 35) for outlines of their character studies.

2) Have the students work from their outlines to create descriptions of the persons whose faces they drew. (The above topics may be arranged in any order. All need not be included.) Encourage the students to work a short anecdote or story into their descriptions to give readers a flavor for the characters.

3) Each student may add a title to the description.

Praising

- Look for words and phrases that give a clear picture of the person.
- Point out sentences that make the character seem interesting, outlandish, or believable.

Polishing

- Instruct the students to delete unnecessary or uninteresting details.
- Students may add active verbs to help describe their characters.
- Have the students add or substitute vivid descriptive words and phrases to build clearer portraits of their characters.

Showing Off

- Let the students display their finished descriptions with their drawings.
- You might want to have the students display their finished descriptions and drawings separately. Let the students try to match the characters with the right characterizations.

Answers To Page 34

#1. MRS. MURKY DESCRIBED IDA DIMPLE, THE LITTLE GIRL WHO HELPED THE VICTIM.
#2. MR. DIMVIEW DESCRIBED MR. SHORTT, THE VICTIM.
#3. MISS TRUESIGHT DESCRIBED BLACKIE BLUE, THE REAL PICKPOCKET.

A Case Of Mistaken Identity

After leaving the barbershop Monday night, Mr. Shortt's wallet was stolen. He caught a shadowy glimpse of the fleeing culprit. A little girl with curly hair and glasses offered to call the police. The police questioned the entire neighborhood and found three witnesses.

Use the Ident-I-Kit and the witnesses' descriptions to draw the suspect. Can you identify the real pickpocket?

I DENT-I-KIT

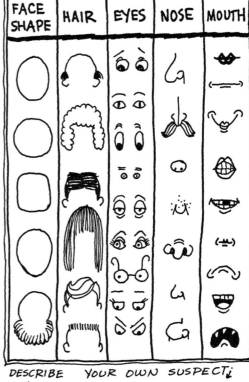

#1. MRS. MURKY DESCRIBED THE PICKPOCKET AS HAVING A ROUND FACE, CURLY BLOND HAIR, GLASSES, SORT OF A PIG NOSE, AND ONE FRONT TOOTH MISSING.

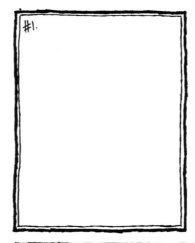

#2. MR. DIMVIEW SAID THE CULPRIT HAD AN OVAL FACE WITH SLEEPY EYES, A LONG NOSE WITH A MUSTACHE, A STRAIGHT THIN MOUTH, AND A BALD HEAD.

DESCRIBE YOUR OWN SUSPECT¡

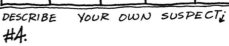
#4.
_____
_____
_____
_____

#3. MISS TRUESIGHT SAID THE PICKPOCKET HAD A SQUARE FACE & A CREW CUT HAIR STYLE. HE HAD TINY, LITTLE EYES AND A NOSE WITH LARGE NOSTRILS. HIS MOUTH WAS SET IN A FROWN.

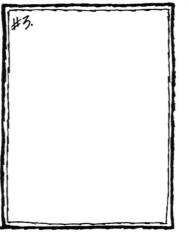

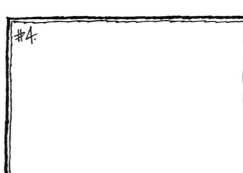

student Page

What's In A Face?

Look carefully at the face you've drawn.

1. Write phrases or words that describe each part of the face you've drawn.

2. Write ideas and phrases to describe the body appearance, size, interesting mannerisms, and dress of the character.

3. Jot down things the character might do -- work, activities, hobbies, habits, places he/she might visit, etc.

4. Write phrases about the character's family and/or friends.

5. Think about the character's personality. Jot down phrases, words, and ideas to describe the character's temperament, moods, outlook on life, etc.

6. Write several possible names for the character.

8. Hold Your Horses!

Materials

- large strip of mural paper with several idioms, to hang on the wall (see example page 39)
- markers or crayons
- tape recorder and blank tapes

Romancing

- Give each student a copy of the student page "Is There A Skeleton In Your Closet?" (page 38), and have the class read the story together.
- Talk to the class about idioms. (Idiom - a group of words that have an "understood" meaning which is different from the meaning the words appear to have.)
- Have the students identify and "translate" the idioms in the story.
- Give the students time to illustrate one of the idioms from the story on the space provided on the student page.

Collecting

- As a class or in small groups, have the students brainstorm to make a list of idioms.
- Students may take turns writing the idioms on the idiom mural with markers or crayons. The idioms should be written large enough to be seen from any spot in the room.

Writing

1) Let the students work as a group, individually, or in pairs to compose stories which contain several idioms.

2) Guide the writing by making these suggestions.

- Choose one idiom as the "theme" of the story. (For example, write a story explaining how and why someone is "in the doghouse".)
- Choose five or more idioms from the mural which might fit into the story.
- Start writing the story and add the idioms as they fit into the plot.
- Try to use an idiom in the final sentence.
- Use an idiom in the title of the story, if possible.

Praising

- Look for clever and interesting uses of idioms.
- Point out effective beginnings and endings.
- Comment on interesting titles.

Polishing

- Have the students examine their stories for clarity. Instruct them to rearrange or replace sentences until the story is clear.

Showing Off

- Students may draw clever illustrations for their stories.
- Provide a time and place for the students to use the tape recorder to record their stories. Compile all the drawings to make a booklet. Place the booklet by the tape recorder so the students can look for the appropriate drawings as they listen to each story. (Label the tapes and drawings so that the students will be able to match them.)

hang tough

don't blow it

keep on an even keel

feather one's nest

chew the fat

knock me over with a feather

Is There A Skeleton In Your Closet?

Everyone thinks I'm the big cheese in math. The real truth is that I have to beat my brains out to get good grades. Today the cat got out of the bag -- everyone saw right through me.

Today was a terrible day. I was down in the dumps from the minute I got out of bed. The first thing that I thought about was the math test that I would have to take at 1:00. My studying last night wasn't worth a hill of beans, and I knew I'd be in a pretty pickle when I got to math class. If that wasn't bad enough, my little brother kept getting in my hair during breakfast. Mom was madder than a wet hen when my little brother and I got into a big fight. She almost bit our heads off! When I left for school it was raining cats and dogs. My bike slipped out from under me and I bit the dust!

When I finally got to school, the math teacher was pretty burned up because none of us turned in our homework. When he handed out the test, I was shaking in my boots. (I know I blew it!) I kept a stiff upper lip at school, but I needed to blow off some steam. I held my tongue until I made it to my room where I could scream my head off and throw things. One of my shoes went through the window, and now I'm really in the doghouse!

How many idioms can you find in the story? Underline them.

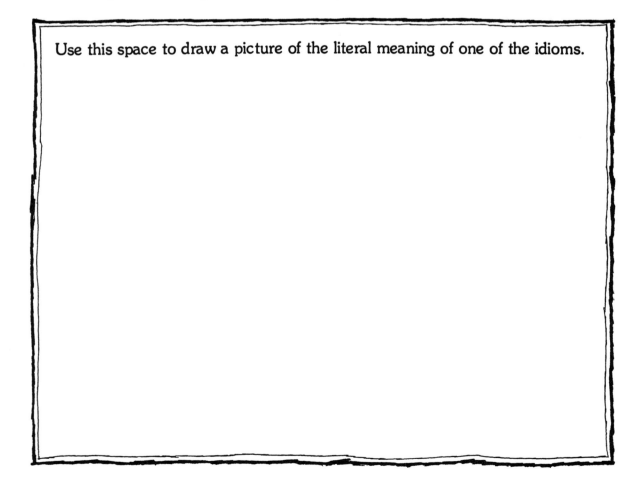

Use this space to draw a picture of the literal meaning of one of the idioms.

Examples

9. What's Up?

PLEASE DON'T ASK, 'WHAT'S UP?'!

Materials

- large pieces of poster board or mural paper (preferably in bright colors) with one of the following words written in the center of each:

RUN OUT SET BACK DOWN TIME FOOT

Romancing

- Distribute copies of the student page "What's Up, Doc?" (page 42).
- Read the story together. Give the students a few minutes to underline and/or count the different uses of the word "up".
- Brainstorm together to add other uses of the word "up".

Collecting

- Have the class work together to gather as many uses as they can for the word "out". Write the uses on the OUT poster.
- Have the class create a short paragraph which uses several of the collected phrases.
- Have the students break into small groups to collect uses for each of the other words on the posters. The students should write the uses for the words on the appropriate posters. They may add uses to the OUT poster, too.

Writing

1) Instruct the students to choose one of the words and to use several of the word's uses in sentences. They may choose to write a story, paragraph, poem, advertisement, news report, etc.

2) The piece of writing must include no less than five uses of the chosen word. Writers will find it challenging to see how many uses they can include, but each writer must make sure the written piece has a theme and makes sense!

Praising

- Look for a variety of uses for the chosen word.
- Point out sentences and phrases that have interesting combinations of uses.
- Look for completed pieces that are understandable.

Polishing

- Instruct the students to include one or more uses of the chosen word in each line or sentence. Have the students reread carefully to see if they can add more uses.
- Have the students break some of their longest sentences into shorter ones.
- Ask the students to strengthen their beginnings or endings. The students may try starting or ending with one of the phrases. (ie: It was *out* of this world!)

Showing Off

- Help the students make a large display with one of the words. Students can draw and design large letters (TIME, for instance) for the center of a bulletin board. Help the students surround the letters with their written pieces containing that word.
- Have the students change the display periodically until all the words and writing examples have been exhibited.

LOOK UP THERE, MOTHER. ANOTHER ONE OF THOSE MIXED-UP KIDS!

What's Up, Doc?

Until now, Clyde Upton has been up to no good. Living alone in his dingy apartment on the sixth floor, Clyde has been up to his ears in debt. In fact, the whole family has been fed up with him for so long that they have just about given up on him.

The family should look him up now, however. A new job has come up for Clyde -- he's moving up in the world. He gets dressed up in a suit each morning, calls the chauffeur, and heads uptown. Once he's in his limousine, he checks on his appointments, writes memos for his secretary, and looks up his stocks in the Wall Street Journal--even when he's tied up in traffic. When the limousine pulls up to the curb, Clyde gets out and climbs up the stairs to his office.

He's building a fortune as an upwardly mobile financier. Several magazines have done a write-up on his overnight success. Clyde's story adds up to this advice. Don't be upset if you're feeling down. Keep your chin up -- you could wind up at the top!

How many different uses of the word "up" can you find in the story? Underline each different use.

Can you think of any ways of using "up" that were not included? Write some other uses below or on the back of this page.

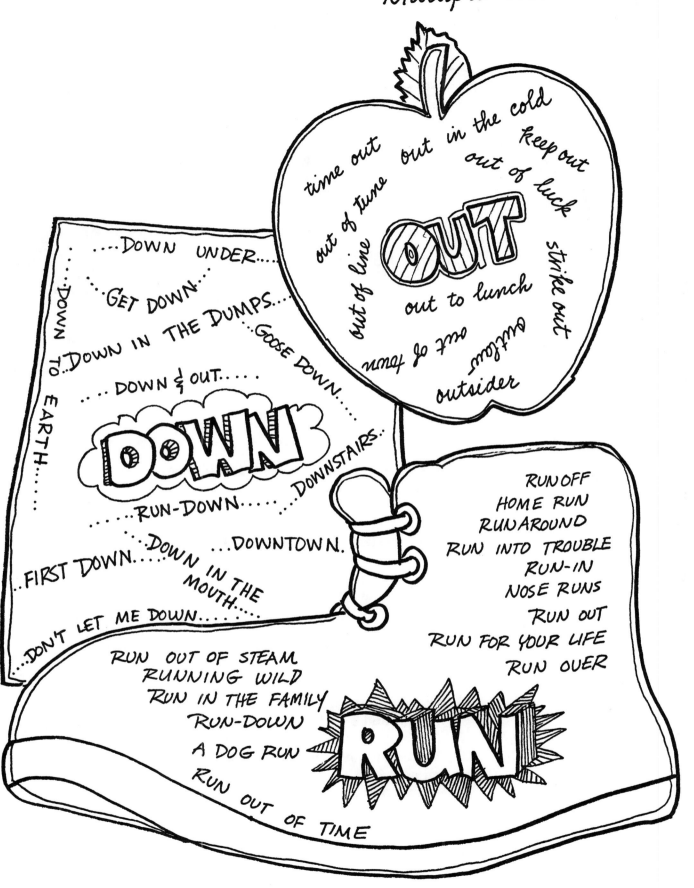

time out · out · in the cold · keep out · out of line · out of tune · out of luck · strike out · out to lunch · out of town · outlaw · outsider

OUT

....DOWN UNDER....
....GET DOWN....
DOWN TO EARTH....
....DOWN IN THE DUMPS....
....GOOSE DOWN....
...DOWN & OUT.....
DOWN
DOWNSTAIRS.
....RUN-DOWN.....
....DOWNTOWN.
...FIRST DOWN.....DOWN IN THE MOUTH....
...DON'T LET ME DOWN......

RUN OFF
HOME RUN
RUN AROUND
RUN INTO TROUBLE
RUN-IN
NOSE RUNS
RUN OUT
RUN FOR YOUR LIFE
RUN OVER

RUN OUT OF STEAM
RUNNING WILD
RUN IN THE FAMILY
RUN-DOWN
A DOG RUN
RUN
RUN OUT OF TIME

Examples

10. Detective Thriller

Materials
- poster board and colored construction paper
- crayons, markers, scissors, glue

Romancing
- Give each student a copy of the student page "Who Done It?" (page 46).
- Give the students time to read the mystery and share their ideas about who committed the crime.

Collecting
- Work together to collect words, names, phrases, and ideas for the following lists:

1) Possible "crimes" needing to be solved
2) Names and brief descriptions of many suspects and detectives (general ideas that might fit any crime)
3) Various motives that a suspect might have for committing a crime
4) Words and phrases that sound mysterious
5) Possible solutions to mysteries

Writing

1) Use the student page "The Case Of The Missing Case" (page 47) to guide writers in collecting ideas for their own detective tales.
2) Suggest that each student include all of the elements of the story mentioned on the student page. The order of the elements can be changed.
3) Go over the directions on the student page with the class. Students may wish to work individually or in pairs.

Praising

- Point out good character descriptions for suspects and detectives.
- Look for phrases, sentences, and words that promote intrigue.

Polishing

- Instruct the students to add words that increase the uncertainty or intrigue.
- Have the students eliminate sentences that are not pertinent to their stories.
- Students should strengthen the characters of the detectives and suspects by adding details to the descriptions.

Showing Off

- Each student may glue the picture of his or her character near the top of a large piece of drawing paper or poster board. (They should label each character.)
- Have the students copy their polished mysteries below the pictures.
- Each student should write the solution to the crime near the bottom of the paper.
- Instruct each student to make a curtain or "door" that conceals the mystery's solution. Readers may open the door to see the solution only after they've tried to solve the mystery on their own!

Who Done It?

At her 4th of July picnic, Ms. Molly McMostess discovers, just after the fireworks display, that all six of her watermelons are missing.

THE SUSPECTS:

BRUISER, THE DOG WHO HAS BEEN SEEN SNIFFING AND STEALING FOOD ALL DAY.

SALLY McMOSTESS, the MISCHIEVOUS DAUGHTER OF HOSTESS MOLLY McMOSTESS.

SLIM FRUITLESS, THE JILTED BOYFRIEND OF SALLY, AND OWNER OF THE FIREWORKS COMPANY.

PRINCESS MUSCLES, THE TOWN'S WEIGHT LIFTING CHAMPION.

LOOIE LIGHTFINGERS, OWNER OF THE GROCERY STORE DOWN THE ROAD.

THE DETECTIVE:

SHIRA SHURELOCK, MASTER CRIME SOLVER !!

THE CLUES:

THE ALIBIS:

- There are watermelon seeds on Bruiser's nose.
- There are watermelon rinds near the area where the fireworks were lit.
- Watermelon prices were cheap at Looie's Grocery the following day.
- Princess Muscles' biceps measured two centimeters bigger on July 5 than on July 3.
- Sally moaned all night with a stomachache.
- Sally was holding her mother's hand during the entire fireworks display.
- Several witnesses swore that Bruiser slept all evening.
- Looie and Princess Muscles were dancing to the music during the fireworks display.
- Slim was busy lighting the fireworks.

WHAT DO YOU THINK?
Who is guilty?
What was the motive?
How did the detective solve the mystery?

The Case Of The Missing Case

This mystery doesn't exist, yet. You must create it!

DESCRIBE THE CRIME:

COMPLETE THE DRAWINGS, NAME AND DESCRIBE THE SUSPECTS:

#1._____ #2._____ #3._____ #4._____

#1._____

_____

#2._____

#3._____

#4._____

_____

DETECTIVE:

_____

NAME AND DESCRIBE THE DETECTIVE. DRAW HIS/HER PICTURE IN THE BOX. ⤴

_____

_____

LIST THE CLUES / POSSIBLE MOTIVES / AND ALIBIS:

Put all of the pieces together and write your own detective thriller. Don't forget to tell "who did it" and how the detective solved the mystery. Use the back of this page.

Student Page

11. Cliff Hangers

Materials
- large drawing paper or colored construction paper
- hangers and masking tape

Romancing
- Read the story "beginnings" on the example page "Stories That Leave You Hanging" (page 51). For each beginning, let the students share ideas about what they think might have happened next and how the story might have ended.
- Talk with the class about the importance and the effect of an interesting beginning.

Collecting
- Hand out copies of the student page "Beguiling Beginnings" (page 50). Discuss examples A, B, C and D. Have the students identify specific reasons why one beginning of each pair is better than the other.
- On the chalkboard, make a list of words and phrases that could be used in the opening of an exciting story. Have the class think about words that imply adventure, suggest mystery, and raise expectations.
- Instruct the students to make the beginnings E, F, G and H stronger. (They should use the list on the board.)
- Help the class collect a list of topics that would be good for "cliff hangers" -- stories that leave readers "hanging".

Writing

1) Each student should choose a topic for a good "cliff hanger" and should write a strong beginning. The openings should be no longer than two or three paragraphs.
2) Remind the writers that their stories must stop at a crucial and exciting place, leaving the ending unknown.
3) Ask the students to invent titles which are catchy but which may fit a variety of endings.

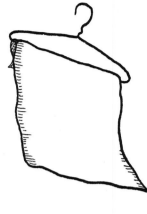

Praising

- Point out words and phrases that leave the reader with a feeling of expectation.
- Comment on words or phrases which include action.

Polishing

- Have the students determine if their stories will leave the reader in suspense. Each student should strengthen the ending sentence by making it more uncertain or exciting.
- Every student should replace inactive verbs or phrases with active ones.
- Have the students delete sentences or ideas that do not contribute to the suspense of a good "cliff hanger".

Showing Off

- The students should copy their stories in large, neat writing on large pieces of drawing paper. (Draw lines on the paper ahead of time.) Have each student leave two inches of space above the title.
- Each student should fold the top edge of the paper over a hanger and then tape the back. Students may hang their "cliff hangers" on a line or wire in the classroom.
- On another day, each student may choose a "cliff hanger", read the beginning, and then finish the story.

Beguiling Beginnings

A. Never before had Tamara dared to open the door at the top of the stairs.

B. One day Tamara decided to go exploring upstairs in her grandmother's house.

C. That day was the windiest day of the year.

D. The wind was so fierce that trees bent to the ground, dishes fell out of cupboards, and 200-pound Mr. McGurdy crashed into the window of Druther's Drug Store.

Improve each beginning below.

E. I was on my way home from school one day when something happened.

F. Last summer I went on the most exciting camping trip of my life.

G. John and Drew were wandering around town one Saturday afternoon. They couldn't think of anything to do.

H. The day of the 6th grade beach picnic had finally arrived. The picnic started off the same as any other class trip.

Mr. Santino was getting ready for the biggest Italian feast he had ever served. Over a hundred dignitaries were having a banquet, and Mr. Santino had been chosen as the caterer because of his great spaghetti.

As the sauce was simmering in a gigantic pot, the spicy aroma filled the kitchen. Since Mr. Santino was busy testing and stirring the sauce, he asked his son, Mario, to put the spaghetti noodles in the pot of boiling water. Mario did not hear his father's directions because he was watching a movie on T.V. Mario put 65 packages of noodles in the pot instead of 25 packages! That was the beginning of the greatest spaghetti disaster in the history of New York.

The two sisters were snooping around the old train station because they had nothing else to do. They had always wondered what was inside the station, but they'd never had the nerve to go exploring until now. The rusty, old train engines were huge, black and fascinating. There was no one around, and so the sisters climbed into the engineer's seat and pretended to drive the powerful engine.

What Susan and Shelly didn't know was that someone else was lurking around the station that day -- someone who had come there to make secret plans. Susan and Shelly were startled when they heard voices inside the station. They hid in the engine, afraid of being caught. What the sisters heard next frightened them even more. They crouched lower to stay out of sight. They probably never would have been noticed if Susan hadn't sneezed.

51

12. EEEErie Tales

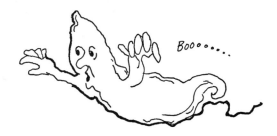

Materials

- tape recorder and cassette tapes

Romancing

- Turn off the lights and close the blinds to create a dark atmosphere. (A dark, stormy day helps!)
- Have the class sit in a circle. Let the students take turns telling scary stories or ghost stories. Page 55 has a few examples.

Collecting

- Give each student a copy of the student page "Things That Go 'Thump' In the Night" (page 54).
- Using the sheet as a guide, the students should collect words, phrases and ideas for each of the categories. The class may work together to brainstorm for these lists, but students should also keep their own lists to help them with the next stage.

Writing

Direct the writing by telling each student to create an eerie story that contains the following.

1) One or two beginning paragraphs that set a scary mood and prepare the reader for something eerie or frightening
2) Two or three paragraphs which detail a mysterious or scary happening
3) An ending of not more than two paragraphs that resolves the mystery, finishes the adventure, or surprises the reader with a "revelation"
4) An ominous, foreboding, or tantalizing title

Praising
- Look for "creepy" words and phrases that help to set the mood.
- Pay special attention to effective beginnings and endings.

Polishing
- Instruct the students to replace or add words that strengthen the spooky effects of their stories.
- Have the students add or rearrange sentences to strengthen the plots of their stories.
- Ask the students to delete unnecessary sentences or sentences that give "secret" information too soon.

Showing Off
- Have the students think of ways to create scary noises to accompany their stories.
- The students can read their stories (in spooky voices) into the tape recorder and accompany the stories with special sound effects.
- Put the tape recorder and the tapes of eerie tales in a closet or dark corner where students can go to listen to the tales.

Things That Go "Thump" In The Night

For each category, list words, phrases, and ideas.

SCARY SOUNDS

CREEPY CREATURES

FRIGHTENING WORDS

MYSTERIOUS WORDS

WORDS THAT "FEEL" DARK

WORDS THAT DESCRIBE A
STRANGE OR SCARY SCENE

ACTION VERBS FOR
EERIE STORIES

WORDS THAT TELL HOW YOU
FEEL IN SCARY SITUATIONS

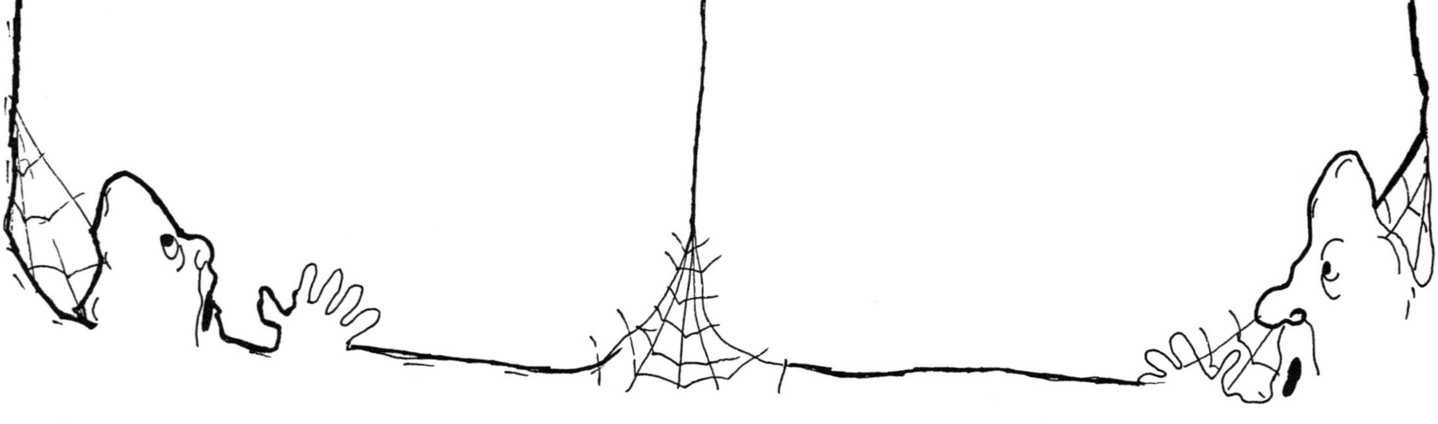

The first time I told my big sister that I heard a strange creature tap-tap-tapping on the window, she said that it was my imagination. Then she heard the sound, but she said it was just the trees scratching against the window. Suddenly, the window began to open and a gnarly, white hand reached into the room. My big sister turned as pale as the thing that was slowly climbing through the window!

The telephone rang at the newspaper office.
"Strange, misty shapes are 'hanging' around the town hall making shrill noises!" a hysterical voice wailed.
"Carter!" yelled the night editor, "Get over to City Hall and check out this story. Maybe you'd better take a ghost-blaster with you . . . some weirdo thinks that there are spirits floating in the air!"

I wondered why Mom and Dad got such a good deal on this house. I know why now -- no one else wanted to live in it! I discovered this the day we moved in the house. My little brother and I followed our parents up the broken, creaking stairs. We walked across a porch filled with cobwebs and then through a heavy, black door. We found ourselves standing in a hall as dark and damp as the inside of a whale!

Examples

13. Modern Mother Goose

Materials
- interesting news articles
- newsprint or poster board
- fine-point black markers or pens

Romancing
- Ask the students to cut out interesting news articles from newspapers to bring to class. Talk about the articles together.
- Tell the students that you have some news items to share. Read the articles on page 58, one at a time, and then ask the students if they recognize the stories.

Collecting
- Group the students in small committees. Ask the committees to examine several news articles and to underline words and phrases that are commonly used by journalists. Remind the students to pay attention to headlines.
- Have the class work together to build a list of these commonly used words.

spectators	witnesses reported
efforts are underway	allegedly
unaccounted-for	officials would
	not say

- Build a list of familiar Mother Goose and/or fairy tale stories.

Writing
1) Each student may choose two Mother Goose rhymes and/or familiar fairy tales.
2) Direct the students to rewrite the rhymes or fairy tales as newspaper reports of present-day happenings.
3) The students may give their stories appropriate headlines, too.

Praising

- Point out eye-catching headlines.
- Compliment students for using words and phrases that sound like newspaper writing.

Polishing

- Each headline should include at least one strong active verb.
- Have the students add more "journalistic" words and phrases to make their stories more like news reports.

Showing Off

- Give the students copies of both student pages labeled "Weekly Reporter" (pages 58 and 59) as models for making their own front pages.
- The students either may write their polished headlines and articles on page 59 (with "photographs" from the scene), or they may make similar front pages from large sheets of newsprint or poster board.

Weekly REPORTER

Bridge Collapses, London Shocked

LONDON (UBI) THE ENTIRE MID-SECTION OF THE FAMOUS BRIDGE BROKE LOOSE AND FELL IN THE THAMES RIVER EARLY TUESDAY MORNING.

WITNESSES REPORTED HEARING CREAKING SOUNDS JUST AFTER 6:30 A.M.

"THERE WAS A LOUD CRACK," SAID ONE SHOCKED MOTORIST, "AND THE AUTO IN FRONT OF ME JUST DISAPPEARED INTO THIN AIR!"

THE EXTENT OF THE CASUALTIES ARE UNKNOWN AT THIS HOUR. RELIABLE SOURCES SAY THERE ARE ESTIMATES OF UP TO 50 PEOPLE MISSING AND PRESUMED DEAD.

WHILE RESCUE EFFORTS ARE UNDERWAY, A GOVERNMENT-APPOINTED COMMISSION HAS BEGUN A THOROUGH INVESTIGATION INTO THE DISASTER.

FIRE DANGER TODAY IS — LOW MED. HIGH EXTREME

staff photo

The London Bridge Disaster

Features

FAIR TONIGHT, LOWS IN THE MID-50's, LIGHT WIND.

Climber Survives Treacherous Fall

(UPI) Yesterday was a lucky day for young Jack Hill of Peaksville. The 12-year-old son of a dentist was descending Black Butte with a heavy bucket about noon when he dropped into a deep crevasse, according to fellow-climber Jill Surefoot.

"I could see that he was adjusting his bucket and not looking ahead. I shouted at him, but he didn't hear me," she told reporters.

Miss Surefoot lowered a rope and managed to pull him out just before he lost consciousness due to severe abrasions to the head. She wrapped his head with some brown paper she had and then left to find help.

Rescuers from the Forest Service reached Hill at 2:00 P.M. and transported him to Humpty Dumpty Hospital for treatment. He is listed in good condition.

staff photo

Young Jack Hill from his hospital bed.

Weekly REPORTER

14. Aesop Revisited

One good turnip deserves another!

Don't jump into the frying pan if you can't take the heat!

Materials
- collections of fables such as AESOP'S FABLES, HESITANT WOLF AND SCRUPULOUS FOX (by Karen Kennerly; Random House), and FABLES FOR OUR TIME (by James Thurber; Harper and Row).
- markers or crayons
- two large Manila envelopes

Romancing
- Read several examples of fables to the class.
- Talk about what a fable is, and let the students tell fables that they have heard.

(A fable is defined as a story intended to teach a useful truth. Fables often include animals who speak and act like human beings.)

60

Collecting

- After listening to several fables, students should begin to compile a list of the kinds of "truths" (or morals) that the fables present. Use the student page "Crafty Foxes and Dancing Grasshoppers" (page 63) as a work sheet for collecting the list.
- Have students add other morals they've heard, or ones they have concocted themselves.

Writing

1) Distribute copies of the student page "Unexpected Lessons" (page 62).
2) Working individually or in pairs, students should choose a moral to communicate. They may use the characters pictured to create a fable which teaches the particular moral.
3) Students might like to create their own characters or to write more than one fable.

Praising

- Share the fables and morals with the class. Point out the fables that clearly present a moral.
- Look for sentences that give the attributes of the characters.

Polishing

- Have the students eliminate any unnecessary phrases or words.
- Students should add descriptive words to strengthen characterizations.
- Ask the students to try including irony in their fables.

Showing Off

- Have the students recopy their fables on clean sheets of paper. They may add illustrations by drawing their own or by cutting and pasting the illustrations on page 62.
- Direct the students to write the morals of their fables on separate, rectangular sheets of paper.
- Mount the fables on a 9" x 11" piece of construction paper and the morals on a half sheet.
- Put the fables in one envelope and the morals in another. Let the students take turns trying to match the morals with the corresponding fables.

He who indulges, bulges!

Don't buy taffy if you have no teeth!

Quit while you're ahead, unless you're behind!

Unexpected Lessons

CHOOSE ONE SCENE FROM ABOVE, OR CREATE YOUR OWN.
WRITE YOUR FABLE HERE.

_____

_____

_____

_____

_____

_____

_____

_____

_____

AND THE MORAL OF THE STORY IS:

_____

Crafty Foxes And Dancing Grasshoppers

A *fable* is a story (usually one that gives animals human qualities) that teaches a moral lesson or promotes a truth.

Some fables are straightforward. Others are ironic. This means that the story may end in a way that is opposite of what you would expect. Many times the person "teaching the lesson" is the one who learns a lesson.

Some fables are silly. Other fables pass on a wise thought.

ADD TO THIS LIST OF "MORALS", "LESSONS", AND BITS OF "WISDOM" THAT FABLES TEACH.

One rotten apple spoils the whole barrel.
Never play with fire.
Crime does not pay.
One who hesitates is sometimes saved.
Don't jump into the frying pan if you can't take the heat.
One good turn deserves another.
Quit while you're ahead.
Two wrongs don't make a right.

_____

_____

_____

_____

_____

_____

GRAPES, MONSIEUR?

THEY'RE PROBABLY SOUR!

MENU

INCLUDE SOME THAT YOU'VE MADE UP!

Don't get out of the boat if you can't swim.
Never trust an alligator that is smiling.
He who indulges, bulges.
Don't buy taffy if you have no teeth.
It is better to have bad breath than no breath at all.
Beware of friends who borrow your toothbrush.
One who climbs flagpoles needs insurance.

_____

_____

_____

_____

_____

_____

_____

STOP FIDDLING YOUR LIFE AWAY!!

Student Page

15. Slightly Stretched

Materials
- adding machine tape, scissors, glue
- large, black construction paper
- books of tall tales (check the library)

Romancing
- Make up a wild, "stretched" story to tell your students, and/or read several tall tales aloud.
- Let the students share their own "whoppers" with the class.

Collecting
- Have the students make a list of "tall tale topics".
- Help the class make a list of good words for exaggeration.

(See the examples below.)

LONG, TALL TOPICS

weather.....
wild creatures...
strange or
    scary animals.
camping trips.....
amusement parks..
teachers I've had..
fast runners.....
fights....
noses.......
strange people...
food .....
fishing trips....
cars/vehicles.....
tests....
accidents...
kids....
scary incidents...
storms.....
waves.....

GOOD WORDS FOR
    LIES........
so tall that...
extraordinary...
never before....
unbelievable....
outlandish...
worst.....
hugest....
horrendous....
a million...
faster than...
impossible...
tremendous...
gasp...
meanest...
longest...
heaviest....
terrible....

64

Look in your library for a wonderful collection of tall tales: WHOPPERS by Alvin Schwarz.

Writing

- Have each student select a topic for a "stretched" story. They may use the student page "Tall, Tall Tales" (page 66) as a springboard for writing.

Praising

- Point out good uses of exaggeration.
- Look for especially humorous or unusual events in the stories.

Polishing

- Ask the students to try to add words that make their stories sound more outlandish.
- Have the students make sure that the story beginnings immediately capture the reader's interest.
- The students should make the endings include something fun, clever, or unexpected.

Showing Off

Direct the students as follows:

- Use black construction paper to create a tall, unusual creature that is an inch or more wider than adding machine tape.
- Paste a strip of adding machine tape on the paper and recopy the tale so that it looks "tall".
- Use extra black paper to make long, tall legs, tall hats, strange noses and arms, etc. Glue these features to the tall creature.

Tall, Tall, Tales

1. Choose a topic for your tale: _____
   (the worst snowstorm ever, a scary camping trip, the wildest roller coaster in the world, etc.)
   Work on an opening sentence that will immediately capture the reader's interest. Examples:

   It's a wonder I'm still alive after last night's camping trip!
   I don't usually ride roller coasters, but the Black Demon is not an ordinary roller coaster!

   _____

   _____

   2. Now write several events that you're going to include in your tale. Don't forget to include words and phrases that are great exaggerations.

3. Number the happenings to put them in an order that will build up to a fantastic ending.
   Write a good ending sentence. Use a big lie, a surprise, something funny, or something that leaves the reader guessing.
   For example:

   The biggest mosquito can carry away a bull single-handedly.

   That was only the first night of the camping trip!

   _____

   _____

The Story of Ben the Baker and the World's Largest Strawberry Shortcake

The Best & Wisest Teacher in the World and What She Did...

How Cowboy Bob Conquered the West...

Examples

16. Whither The Weather?

THE CLOUD PEOPLE MUST BE PEELING ONIONS TODAY.

Materials
- markers, crayons, charcoal, and/or colored construction paper
- large drawing paper
- scissors and glue
- collections of myths from the library

Romancing
- Talk about unusual, interesting, or frightening weather patterns. (During or after a storm or some other weather "occurrence" is a good time to do this!)
- Define a myth and explain how people have made up stories to explain natural happenings that they couldn't understand (such as the weather). Read a few myths to the students.
- Have the students use art media such as charcoal, crayons, paints, markers, and torn paper to create pictures of various weather patterns. As the students work, they should think about mythical explanations for their weather "happenings".

Collecting

- Hand out copies of the student page "Weather Update" (page 70), and have the class work together to add to the list of weather ideas.
- Let the students brainstorm in pairs or small groups to generate answers to the questions at the bottom of the student page. Have each pair or group share their ideas with the whole class to demonstrate the possibilities for weather myths.
- Ask the students to choose topics for original weather myths. The students can write the myths on their own copies of the student page "Weather Myths" (page 71), and then write brief summaries of their explanations.
- Direct the students to collect words and phrases to be used in their myths.

Writing

- Each student should begin writing a weather myth, expanding on the summarized explanation and including the collected words and phrases. The students may:

  1) Explain what causes a certain weather "occurrence".
  OR
  2) Tell what circumstances brought about the first typhoon, snowfall, etc.

Praising

- Look for interesting and unusual mythical characters or "forces".
- Point out strong, catchy titles.

Polishing

- Often such tales become too long and burdensome. Have the students tighten and shorten their myths by eliminating unnecessary or dull sentences.
- Ask the students to add dialogue, if possible.

Showing Off

- Create a bulletin board display called "Whither The Weather?" using the finished weather myths and pictures.

OR

- Combine the weather myths and pictures to make a book which can be donated to the school library.

Weather Update

Add your ideas to this list of weather-related happenings.

rain	thunder	thunderstorms
lightning	hail	snowflakes
snowfall	blizzard	ocean waves
sandstorm	fog	typhoon
hurricane	tornado	sunshine
moon	tides	wild wind
soft breezes	mist	sunrise
sunset	season changes	clouds

_____   _____

_____   _____

_____   _____

What do you think?

What creature or character caused the first blizzard?
Who drags the hot, heavy sun into the sky each morning? How?
When was the first time a breeze blew over the ocean?
What kind of weather might have been started by a tug-of-war between two giants?
Who thought of making hail and for what purpose was it created?
What makes clouds move?
What two arguing characters might be responsible for the tides?
Why is the sea sometimes calm and sometimes angry?

Weather Myths

Choose a topic for a weather myth.

(Example: Why does the sun seem to be hotter during the summer?)

_____

Write a brief summary of your explanation.

    Example: When a giant warrior did not follow the commands of his general, the god of fire, the warrior was required to carry a large burning ball to the top of a mountain and hold the ball above the earth for 100 days each year.

_____

_____

_____

_____

_____

Collect words and phrases that describe the action, appearance, sound, etc. of this kind of weather.

Examples: scorching; fiery fingers; steaming muscles; trudging steps; burning streaks; yellow, crackling sphere; aching back; strong, powerful legs

Use the words and phrases you've collected to write a complete myth. (You can use the back of this page.)

17. On The Track Of Bigfoot

AN INVITATION TO:

Materials

- large invitation, prepared ahead of time (use the pattern on page 75)
- colored construction paper or poster board
- crayons, markers, scissors, glue, and other art materials needed for making invitations

Romancing

- Show the class the invitation that "mysteriously" appeared in your classroom.
- Read the invitation together and talk about Bigfoot. Let the students share what they've heard about the creature.

Collecting

- Instruct the students to pay special attention to the components of the invitation. The class should make a list of general invitation components. Each student may write a list on the student page "You're Invited!" (page 74). The class may add components other than those found on the "Bigfoot" invitation.

  Example: description of event, location, date, time, directions, what to bring, what to wear, host or hostess, charge (if any), etc.

- Have the class brainstorm to make a list of many kinds of invitations, as well as places and events for gatherings or parties.

Writing

1) Each writer should choose one event to which someone could be invited.
2) Using the collected components, each student should write the information needed to complete an invitation.

Praising

- Point out interesting and unusual choices of events, locations, and other pieces of information given in the invitations.
- Look for special words and phrases which contribute to the mood or atmosphere of the event.

Polishing

- Have the students check their invitations for completeness. They should make sure that all of the important information is included.
- Ask the students to add words or phrases that create humor, suspense, or anticipation.

Showing Off

- Have the students write their information on large invitations of various shapes.
- Encourage the students to be imaginative in designing their invitations.
- Encourage the students to share their invitations with other classmates and other classes.

You're Invited!

What information is needed in an invitation? Make a list below.

What kinds of invitations would you like to receive?

What kinds of invitations would you like to send?

Think of some really outlandish invitations.
Write them below.

Come Follow Bigfoot!

JOIN THE ANNUAL Bigfoot Hunting Expedition
See the Creature For YOURSELF!
(Get your picture taken with a Sasquatch!)

WHO MAY JOIN - All bold, curious Bigfoot lovers over age 10

WHERE MEET AT HAIRY TOE JUNCTION 7:00 A.M. - JULY 17th

HOW LONG UNTIL WE FIND ONE!!! searchers may join for any period from 1 week to all summer!

LEADERS - DR. DON WILL FINDER and DR. MARY A. HUNTER (the world's most experienced Sasquatch hunters!)

BRING - STURDY BOOTS, NEUTRAL CLOTHING, CAMERA, FOOD, WATER BOTTLE, FLASHLIGHT, AND PLENTY OF NERVE !!!

DON'T BRING - GUNS OR MARSHMALLOWS. (BIGfoot goes WILD in the presence of marshmallows!)

MAP

Footprint Pass
MYTHICAL HWY.
HAIRY TOE JUNCTION
Hwy 66
Monster Rd.

SPONSORED BY THE UNIVERSAL BIGFOOT SOCIETY

Use this as a pattern to make your own "Bigfoot" invitation to share with your class.

Teacher Pattern

18. You'd Better Watch Out

Materials

- poster board
- crayons or markers
- construction paper
- scissors and glue

Romancing

- Read or recite several poems or other kinds of warnings. For example:

  "Warning" and "Early Bird" from WHERE THE SIDEWALK ENDS, by Shel Silverstein.
  "Grizzly Bear" by Mary Austin, from TIME FOR POETRY, edited by Mary Hill Arbuthnot.

Collecting

- Have the class tell stories about some of the things they have been warned to do or not to do.
- Tell the students to make lists on the student page "Warnings" (page 78) of things they've been warned not to do, say, eat, etc. Collect the lists as a class.
- Have the class discuss possible consequences for various unheeded warnings.
- Encourage the class to collect silly or outlandish warnings.

EAT YOUR VEGETABLES

*If you don't eat
your vegetables,
this is what
will happen:
Your head will turn
into a green pepper,
Your toes will turn
to peas,
Your nose will turn
into a banana squash,
And beans will
grow out of
your knees!*

Writing

Let the students work in pairs or as individuals to do either of the following:

1) Write a list (or poem) of several warnings, each one accompanied by a consequence.

   Starters: Be careful not to _____
   If you should _____
   Don't ever _____
   Always _____
   Never, never _____
   Always remember to _____

2) Write one warning in more detail, expanding in prose or poetry form why you should or shouldn't follow the warning and the possible consequences.

Praising

- Look for familiar and "fun" warnings, as well as interesting consequences.
- Point out words and phrases that suggest a cautious feeling or that make a consequence seem undesirable.

Polishing

- Instruct the students to break up any sentences that are too long or awkward. Have the students rework some sentences to give a variety of lengths and structures.
- Students should try to exaggerate one or more of the consequences.

Showing Off

- Have the students use crayons, markers, or paint to create a large "warning poster". The poster should include one warning, its consequence, and an illustration.

Warnings!!

Don't climb that high tree,
You'll surely get hung on a branch.
Leaves will get stuck in your ears,
And birds will drop plops on you!

Things you've been warned not to do:

DON'T LISTEN TO LOUD MUSIC OR YOUR BRAINS WILL BECOME MUSH!

NEVER PLAY WITH ELECTRICITY IN THE BATHTUB.

Things you've been warned to do:

ALWAYS WATCH BOTH WAYS BEFORE CROSSING THE STREET!

ALWAYS TIE YOUR SHOELACES, OR YOU'LL TRIP OVER YOUR OWN FEET!

Don't say you haven't been
WARNED!

WARNING!

If you cross your eyes,
They'll probably stick.

If you eat with dirt
under your fingernails,
You'll become sick!

WARNING TO ELEPHANT LOVERS

Never tickle an elephant,
For when an elephant
begins to
Grin, cackle, laugh and
giggle,
An elephant begins to
topple...
And you never want to be
close to a falling
elephant!

YOU SHOULD KNOW BETTER

Don't ever put watermelon
seeds
In your nose or your ears,
Or you'll have a melon patch
On your head in a few years.

Your skull will turn green
And form stripes like a rind,
And sticky pink juice
Will drip out of your mind!

79

Examples

19. It's A Great Buy

Materials
- ads from magazines, newspapers, or other sources
- drawing paper, colored construction paper
- markers and crayons
- scissors and glue

Romancing
- Make a collection of ads. (Students can look for ads ahead of time and contribute to the collection.)
- Read the ads aloud. Have the students talk about other ads they have seen on T.V. or billboards.

Collecting
- Have the class try to identify common elements in the ads. Make a list of the elements:

  ie: - the ads make you feel that you're missing something
        - the ads give promises
        - the ads describe a product in very appealing terms

- Have the class make another list of words and phrases which can be used to describe products.
- Help the class make a third list of advantages of owning certain products.

TRAVELING SALESMAN "EVERYTHING you always wanted"

Writing

1) Hand out copies of the student page "You've Got To Have This!" (page 82). Read the ads on page 83 to the students.

2) Each student should choose two of the products pictured on page 82 and create an advertisement for each. Remind the students to make use of the words, phrases, and ideas already collected. The students can write the ads in the spaces provided at the bottom of the student page.

Praising

- Point out clever, catchy words and phrases that convince people to buy the product.
- Point out strong words and phrases that make the product appealing.

Polishing

- Have the students add convincing words to strengthen their ads.
- Instruct the students to add phrases or words that make the reader certain the product is a good one.

Showing Off

- Have the students transfer their ads to large posters or magazine-sized paper and create full color ads, complete with written copy and illustrations.
- Show off the ads on a bulletin board or other display.

You've Got To Have This!

STOP SOLICITORS SHORT!

are you bugged by bothersome peddlers of junk?

YOUR TROUBLES ARE OVER.

LIVE THE QUIET LIFE YOU LIKE WITH THE NEW SALESMAN-BITING DOG. (GUARANTEED)

Grrrrrrr

THE RUSHING FLUSH IS MUSIC TO YOUR EARS

NEVER FRET AGAIN OVER CLOGS AND SLOGS IN BOWLS AND DRAINS

POP'S "POWER" PLUNGER

gets things going again!!

POP!   POP!

100% safe & odor-free

THE FIBER YOU NEED WITH THE FLAVOR YOU CRAVE.

CRISPIE NIPPIES CEREAL

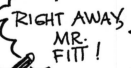

CRUNCHY, CRACKLY, GOOD OAT FLAKES SPRINKLED WITH TACO-FLAVORED NUGGETS THAT NIP YOUR TONGUE DELIGHTFULLY!!!

100% R.D.A of FIBER

HAVEN'T YOU GOT THOSE ADVERTISING POSTERS DONE YET?

RIGHT AWAY, MR. FITT!

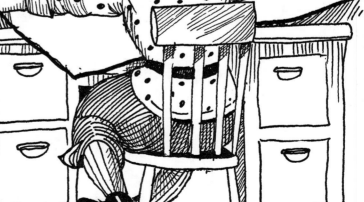

Examples

20. Ghastly Giggles

Materials
- large bulletin board or mural paper (preferably black)
- construction paper, scissors, glue

Romancing
- Share several "ghostly jokes and riddles" by giving each student a copy of the example page "Guides to Ghastly Giggles" (page 87).
- Give the students time to tell other ghost, goblin, spook, and vampire-related puns and riddles.

Collecting
- Brainstorm to make the following lists, using the student page "A Collection of Spooks" (page 86) as a springboard.
  - words that have to do with graveyard characters, spooks, or scary occurrences
  - phrases that are puns on "spooky" words and make good punch lines for jokes or answers to riddles

Writing

1) Have the students work individually or in pairs to write two or more "ghostly" riddles or jokes.
2) Encourage the students to make use of their collected ideas for punch lines and riddle answers.

Praising

- Enjoy laughing at unexpected wordplays and silly answers.

Polishing

- Instruct the students to make sure that their questions or jokes are written as complete, clear sentences.

Showing Off

- Have the students create "graveyard" creatures from white, silver, orange, yellow, grey, red, and green paper.
- Display the "creatures" with the riddles and jokes on a bulletin board or mural. Make one large "ghastly" scene.

A Collection Of Spooks

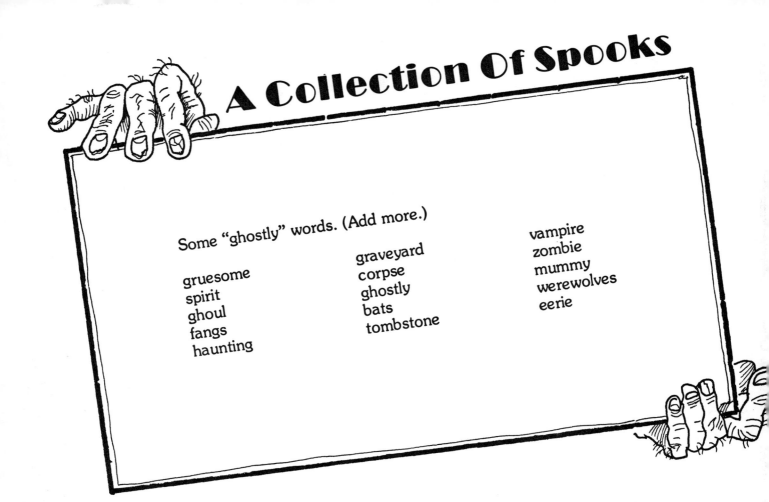

Some "ghostly" words. (Add more.)

gruesome
spirit
ghoul
fangs
haunting

graveyard
corpse
ghostly
bats
tombstone

vampire
zombie
mummy
werewolves
eerie

Possible punch lines or riddle solutions. (Add more.)

a *horrorscope*
blood *vessels*
a *coffin* break
the Dead Sea
an undercover agent
a ghost writer
because he wanted to find
   out his blood type
a ghost on fire
"I want my mummy!"

*ghoul*ash
*fangs*giving
a roller *ghoster*
in a blood bank
a *ghost-to-ghost* flight
"a-*haunting* we will go"
a tombstone
he could feel it in his
   bones
a wash-and-*werewolf*

Write your own ghastly joke or riddle here:

_____

_____

_____

Examples—Guides To Ghastly Giggles

21. Straight To The Future

Materials
- crayons or markers
- Manila envelopes (9" x 12" or smaller)
- masking tape or sealing wax
- book or story about the future

Romancing
- Read a story about the future to the class. (optional)
- Talk with the students about books, movies, or stories they've read or seen about the future.
- Ask the students to tell what they think life will be like 10 or more years in the future.
- Give each student a copy of the student page "What A Future!" (page 90), and ask the students to draw scenes from the future.

Collecting
- Let the students share drawings and ideas about the future world.
- Have the students collect lists of words and phrases that can be used to describe the futures of the following:
  - homes
  - toys
  - schools
  - jobs
  - towns
  - sports
  - cars and other transportation
  - food
  - music and music devices
  - landscapes
  - shopping centers
  - recreational activities

Writing
1) Ask the students to pretend that they've been "zoomed" into the future by a fantastic time machine.
2) Have each student write a diary entry about his or her day in the future. The student should describe the events of the day, including as much about the future world as may fit in three or four paragraphs.
3) Remind the students to date their entries.

Praising
- Point out imaginative inventions and ideas about the future.
- Look for variety in the day's events. Comment on the completeness of the entries.

Polishing
- Ask the students to look for words, phrases, and ideas that can be replaced with more fantastic or inventive ones.
- Students should delete any sentences that do not add information or excitement to their entries.

Showing Off
Share the drawings and diary entries now and in the future! Here's how:
- Create a class booklet or bulletin board to display the drawings and the diary entries. Entitle the booklet or board "Straight To The Future".
- Have each student complete the student page "Time Capsule" (page 91).
- Have each student put the diary entry, future drawing, and "Time Capsule" page into an envelope. Instruct the students to seal their envelopes well (preferably with sealing wax) and to write the following information on the front:

Time Capsule
Do Not Open
Until January 1, _____
(choose the date)

- Have each student take his or her time capsule home and store it in a safe place.

What A Future!

What will things look like in the future? Draw a scene that might be found in the year
_____ . (You fill in the blank!)

Use the back of this page to write your diary entry describing your visit to the future.

Time Capsule

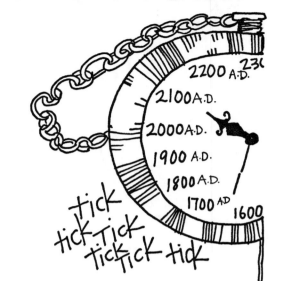

A time capsule is a fantastic thing to discover. It tells you what things were like in the past. You are going to make a time capsule today. Complete this page to put inside the capsule with some other things you choose. This information will tell the you of the future what you are like today. (No one will see this except you!)

Today's date is _____ .

I am _____ years old and I am in the _____ grade.

What I like to do most is _____ .

These people are important to me: _____ .

I'm good at _____ .

What I value most is _____ .

I worry about _____ .

I get angry about _____ .

Recently, I've learned _____ .

Ten years from now, I hope I _____ .

Something I'd like to accomplish in my life is _____

_____ .

Something special about me is _____ .

Put this page in your time capsule with your drawing of the future, your future diary entry, and anything else you'd like. Choose a date to open the capsule and write it on the outside of the capsule.

Student Page

22. To A Rollercoaster . . .

Materials
- long piece of mural paper
- pencils, crayons, markers, paints

Romancing
- Ask the class to talk about roller coaster rides and other "wild ride" experiences they've had.
- Read the ode examples on page 95.
- Talk about odes. (For the purposes of this activity, "ode" can be defined loosely as a piece of poetry or prose that is addressed to someone or something, and which speaks with great feeling or respect.)
- Ask the students to think about what they would say to a roller coaster.

Collecting
- As a class, make a list of words and phrases that have to do with wild rides. Include the following:
    - feelings and fears that you get when riding on a wild ride
    - descriptions of the cars, track, etc.
    - reasons you love (or hate, or fear) wild rides

WRITING
- Have the class work together, individually or in pairs, to write a poem or paragraph addressed to a roller coaster (or other wild ride).
  Direct the students as follows:
1) Work on an opening line that is catchy and lets the reader know immediately how you feel about the roller coaster.
2) Give the ride a name and the poem or paragraph a title.
3) Write several other sentences or lines that tell:
    - why you feel a certain way about the ride
    - what the ride's special characteristics are
    - what is fun, scary, admirable, or powerful about the ride
4) Write a closing sentence that gives a concluding thought or feeling.

TO MY ERASER

Oh, Eraser on my pencil top,
I chomp on you and cannot stop.
How many times have I had this fit,
I try, but I just cannot quit.

As soon as one mistake's erased
I hunger for your spongy taste.

"No more!" my mind says, "Quit, you fool!"

But then my mouth begins to drool.

The pencil rises on its own
And then I feel you at my tongue.

My teeth bite in until they meet

And soon you're lying at my feet.

92

Praising
- Look for words and phrases that express how the student feels about the roller coaster.
- Point out words and phrases that are vividly descriptive of the roller coaster.

Polishing
- Have the students add imagery to the poems or paragraphs.
- Instruct the students to rearrange sentences or lines to make their pieces build in feeling.

Showing Off
- Let the students use various art media to design a huge roller coaster on a long piece of mural paper.
- Hang the roller coaster on a wall and display the finished odes beside it.

More Odes
- Repeat the writing process so that the students may write other odes. The student page "Oh, Oh, It's An Ode" (page 94) will guide the students.

Oh, Oh, It's An Ode

Make a list of some of the things to which you could write an ode. Here are some examples. Add your own ideas!

- to an old sneaker
- to your childhood
- to the end of summer
- to a thunderstorm
- to a math test

- to a sunburn
- to peanut butter
- to yesterday
- to your stereo
- to a motorcycle

_____   _____

_____   _____

_____   _____

_____   _____

Follow these steps to write an ode.

1) Choose a person, place or thing to which you want to speak.
2) Write phrases that tell how you feel about this person, place or thing, and why you feel this way.
3) Write several phrases that describe special qualities of your subject.
4) Write phrases that explain why your subject is important to you, or what your subject brings to mind.
5) Combine some of your phrases into lines for a poem or sentences for a paragraph.
6) Review the lines or sentences you've written.
   - Eliminate any lines or sentences that are too much alike.
   - Add more feeling to any weak lines or sentences.
   - Choose a good beginning line or sentence.
   - Number the lines or sentences in the best order.
   - Choose a strong ending line or sentence -- one which clearly expresses how you feel about your subject.
7) Rewrite your ode with the revisions you've just made. Illustrate your ode with a picture, photograph, or concrete object. Share your ode and illustration with your classmates.

TO SEPTEMBER

I've dreaded your arrival,
Looked forward to you, too.
Oh, month of new beginnings,
I'm glad, yet scared, of you.

New classes, new teachers,
New chances, new shoes,
Old worries, old habits,
Old friends with new news.

You bring each one back.
I'm nervous you're here,
And excited, September,
You start the school year.

MY CHICKEN POX

To chicken pox,
Your polka dots
Have left me
Full of fancy spots.

From head to toe,
And, do you know,
I've counted 300,
And there's more to go!

I'm red and white.
I itch all night.
Be done with me!
Please stop this fight.

Goodbye spots
   and itchy socks.
Go to Mars.
Don't leave scars.
Goodbye, goodbye
   to chicken pox!

23. Of Lizards And Leprechauns

Green is the quiet of
   a secret garden,
The smell of mint,
A cricket's chirp,
Pickles,
And a leprechaun.

Green is the mountains
   and algae-filled ponds,
Happiness and mold.
It's the feeling you
   get when you have
   the flu.

Green is sour.
It's broccoli and
   lizards, celery
and loneliness.

Cold is green,
And frostbite.
Green is lime
And crunchy salads.

Materials
- colored chalk
- spray fixative
- newspaper
- large, white drawing paper
- colored construction paper
- Mary O'Neill's HAILSTONES AND HALIBUT BONES

Romancing
- Tell the students ahead of time to wear green for this activity.
- *Optional:* Read a few selections from HAILSTONES AND HALIBUT BONES, by Mary O'Neill.
- Give each student a piece of drawing paper and colored chalk. Ask each student to cover the paper with a design (*not a picture*) that is predominantly green. (Other colors may add contrast, but green must dominate.)
- Ask the students to think about green objects, feelings, experiences, smells, sounds, and ideas as they work.

Collecting
- Ask the following questions. Work as a class to make lists of green words, phrases, and ideas.

    List 1   What things *look* green?
    List 2   What things *sound* green?
    List 3   What things *smell* green?
    List 4   How does green *feel*?
    List 5   What makes *you feel* green?
    List 6   What things *taste* green?
    List 7   What *experiences* or *ideas* seem green?
    List 8   Can you think of any green *places*?

Writing
1) Give each student a copy of the student page "Green...Green...Green" (page 98) as a guide for writing.
2) Encourage the students to select ideas from their lists and to add new ideas as they complete lines.

Praising
- Look for phrases or ideas that have strong sensory appeal.
- Point out unusual comparisons and correlations to the color green.

Polishing
- Have the students add at least one line that creates a good visual image.
- Students should check the order of lines for interest and flow, rearranging lines when necessary. Direct the students to make sure they've chosen good beginning and ending lines.
- Students should give their "green" poems imaginative titles.

Showing Off
- Help the students spray fixative on their chalk designs and mount the designs on construction paper frames.
- Instruct the students to recopy their poems. Mount the poems on green construction paper and affix the poems to the front or back of the chalk designs.

More Color Poetry
- Have the students choose other colors as subjects for individual poems and designs. Display the finished products in a classroom "color gallery".
- Students may "stray" from the form on page 98. Encourage the students to create new lines for their color poems. *Note:* This activity is wonderful for accompanying a science unit on color and light.

I KNOW I'M JUST A GREEN CUB REPORTER — BUT THAT LOOKS LIKE A LEPRECHAUN TO ME!

_____ (title)

Green is _____ and _____ (from list 1)

and _____ . (from list 4)

Green is the taste of _____ . (from list 6)

_____ and _____ smell green. (list 3)

_____ makes me feel green. (list 5)

Green is the sound of _____ and _____ . (list 2)

Green is _____ , _____ , and

_____ . (from list 8)

_____ is green. (from list 7)

_____ is also green. (from list 7)

Green is _____ . (from any list)

Add lines of your own:

Feel free to change or rearrange any of these ideas. Put your ideas together in your own way. When you have revised and rearranged, recopy or type your finished poem.

YELLOW

Yellow never wants help,
But steps right out on its own,
Throwing bright light everywhere.

Yellow dashes through flower gardens,
Splashes on fried eggs,
Drips on traffic lights,
And wraps itself around bananas.

Yellow reaches out from the sun,
And never gives up.

Yellow is BOLD.

BROWN

Brown is a brownie,
And brown is my dog.
Brown is a chocolate shake.
Boxes are brown.
Root beer is brown.
Foxes are brown, too.
Brown is a winter day.
Brown is a frown.
Brown is gingerbread baking.
Homework is brown.

Having to get up and go to school
in the morning,
Getting into fights with your
friend,
Eating something you don't like—
All of these are brown.

Being punished is brown.
Brown is getting warm on a
cold day,
Or having your foot fall asleep.

Examples

24. Opulent Opposites

HOT
Warm, Sticky
Melting, Sweating, Thirsting
SUN, STEAM, ICE, SNOW
Cooling, Shivering, Freezing
Numb, Frosty
COLD

SAD
LONELY, WEEPY
CRYING, WISHING, MISSING
HURT, TEARS, SMILES, JOY
LEAPING, LAUGHING, CLAPPING
EXCITED, CHEERY
GLAD

Materials
- cardboard or poster board
- scissors, glue, crayons, markers
- lots of old magazines
- aluminum foil
- string, hole punch

Romancing
- As a group, think of as many pairs of opposite words (or ideas) as you can. Write the word pairs on the chalkboard.
- Have the students look through magazines for pictures of opposites (example: day and night, hot and cold). Students can work together in small groups.
- Instruct the students to cut, trim, and label the pictures.

Collecting
- Ask each student to choose a pair of opposites (preferably a pair for which pictures have been found). You may wish to let some or all of the students work with a partner.
- Direct the students to collect words and ideas for each of the opposite words as directed on the student page "As Opposite As Night And Day" (page 102). Guide the students through each step of collecting. Write a pair of opposites on the board or overhead projector so that the students can see how the collecting is done.
- Students may contribute ideas to each other at this stage.

Writing
1) Guide the students through the steps outlined on the student page "A Diamond Of Opposites" (page 103).
2) Work on your own diamante on the board as the students write diamantes on their papers.

SMOOTH
SILKY, SOFT
SLIDING, SOOTHING, STROKING
GLASS, MILK SHAKE, SPLINTER, GRAVEL
SCRATCHING, PRICKING, STUMBLING
LUMPY, ROCKY
ROUGH

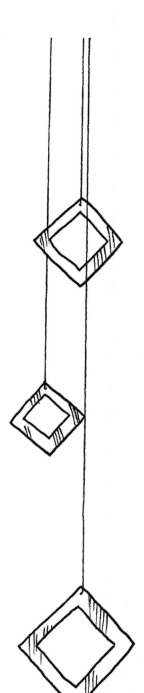

Praising

- Point out appealing or unusual word choices.
- Look for combinations and sequences of words that have particularly pleasant sounds.

Polishing

- Taking one line at a time (lines 2, 3, 4, 5, 6), ask the students these questions:
    - Do you like the words you've chosen?
    - Is there another word that would sound better or that would be more interesting?
    - How do the words sound together?
    - Would the words sound better if they were rearranged?
- Give the students time to replace and rearrange each line.

Showing Off

- Cut a diamond shape for each student from cardboard or poster board.
- Cover the shapes on both sides with foil.
- Instruct each student to copy his or her diamante poem neatly, trim the poem in a diamond shape, and mount the poem on one side of the cardboard diamond.
- Have the students glue the pictures which show the opposites on the other side of the diamond. (The students may make a collage of several pictures, if they wish.)
- Punch a hole in the top of each diamond and suspend the diamonds from the ceiling with string.

As Opposite As Night And Day

Choose a pair of opposites. _____ and _____

A.

List *adjectives* which describe the first word.

B.

List *participles* (ing verbs) related to the first word.

C.

List *nouns* related to the first word.

D.

List *nouns* related to the second word.

E.

List *participles* (ing verbs) related to the second word.

F.

List *adjectives* which describe the second word.

A Diamond Of Opposites

Follow the outline below to write a diamante.

Line 1   _____   the first word in the pair of opposites

Line 2   _____ , _____   two adjectives from list A

Line 3   _____ , _____ , _____   three participles from list B

Line 4   _____ , _____ , _____ , _____
      (two nouns from list C) (two nouns from list D)

Line 5   _____ , _____ , _____   three participles from List E

Line 6   _____ , _____   two adjectives from list F

Line 7   _____   the second word in the pair of opposites

103

25. Outdoor Observation

THE ORANGE MOON... SO BIG SO SILENT

SOME TRIBES OF HIMALAYANS WRITE PRAYERS ON ROUGH PAPER AND HANG THEM ON BRANCHES. AS THE PAPER DISINTIGRATES IN THE WIND, THEY FEEL THAT THEIR WORDS ARE CARRIED TO HEAVEN.

THE TREE'S BARK IS HOME TO TINY CREATURES.

Materials
- brown paper grocery sacks
- jute twine, hole punch, scissors
- black India ink (or other permanent ink)
- large poster board
- marker

Romancing
- Take the class for an outdoor walk or some other quiet excursion. (After a rainstorm, during a snowfall, in the early morning, and on a windy day are especially good times to do this.)
- Spend about a half hour listening to outdoor sounds, watching natural "happenings", and smelling and feeling the out-of-doors.

Collecting
- After finding a spot to sit together, collect words and phrases that describe outdoor feelings, sounds, sights, smells, tastes, experiences, or ideas.
- Have the students write as many of these words and phrases as they can on large pieces of poster board. (Do this outdoors, if possible.)

Writing
1) Have the class work together to write a few thoughts about the out-of-doors or the weather. Each thought should be no more than 10 words and need not be a complete sentence.
2) Tell the students that there is a special written "saying" called a weathergram -- a short, nature thought which one hangs outdoors to let the weather "finish". Read some examples of weathergrams from page 107.
3) Ask each student to write one or more short thoughts that are in some way connected to the outdoors, seasons, or weather. Each thought must be 10 words or less.
4) Place the collected lists on poster board and display them in a prominent place. Give each student a copy of the student page "How To Start A Weathergram" (page 106) on which to write a rough draft.

Praising

- Point out new ideas.
- Comment on poems that relate a feeling you've experienced before.
- Comment on good "outdoor" words.

Polishing

- Instruct the students to eliminate any unnecessary words.
- Ask the students to add at least one word that communicates action.
- Remind the students to include sensory words.

Showing Off

- Have the students follow the directions for making weathergrams found on page 106.
- Let the students hang their weathergrams outdoors to be "finished" by the weather.

How To Start A *Weathergram*

A *weathergram* is a thought that you write and the weather "finishes"! Weathergrams are poems (10 words or less) that are written with permanent ink on biodegradable materials. Begin your weathergram here and follow the directions below to "finish" it.

_____

_____

_____

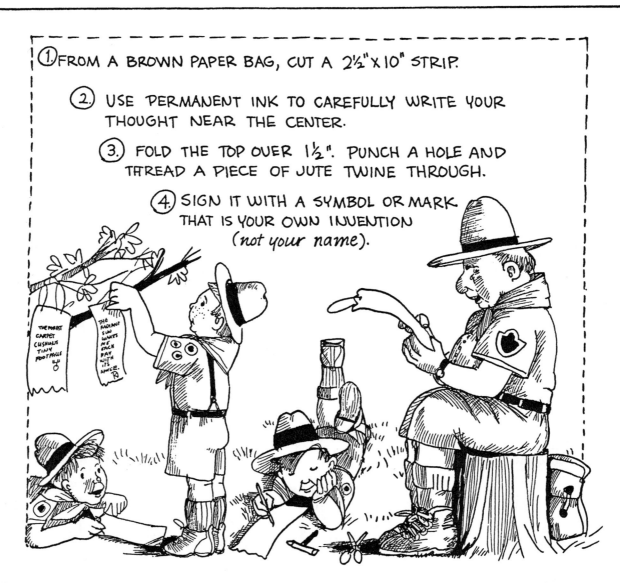

Hang your weathergram outdoors in a place where passers-by can enjoy your thought. The sun, rain, wind, and snow will "finish" your weathergram in approximately three months. Weathergrams do not spoil the environment but blend with their surroundings, eventually decomposing and returning to nature.

Examples

26. I'm Bugged!

Materials
- strip of paper about 12 inches wide and five or six feet long
- hanger or wooden dowel with string
- markers

Romancing
- Have the class sit in a circle. Begin a discussion by telling the students a few things that really "bug" you. You might start each sentence by saying, "I just hate it when..."
- Go around the circle and let the students voice their own "pet peeves".
  Note: This activity helps to dissipate frustration and anger!

Collecting
- Tell the students to write several "pet peeves" on their copies of the student page "Don't You Just Hate..." (page 110).
- Let the students chat while they are writing to help generate more ideas.

Writing

Guide the students through the following steps for writing individual poems.
1) Select eight or more of your best ideas. (Eliminate any that are dull or too much like other ones.)
2) Write each "pet peeve" as a line for a poem.
3) Choose an appropriate line for a good beginning or add a new line. Do the same for the ending.
4) Arrange the lines in the best order.
5) Choose a title that lets the reader know that you're "bugged" about something.

Praising

- Point out amusing lines and "pet peeves" that are commonly shared. (A reader finds it satisfying to realize he or she shares a feeling with the writer.)
- Comment on interesting and unique titles.

Polishing

- Have the students rearrange lines for effectiveness.
- Students should try to add words or phrases that communicate their indignant feelings concerning their "pet peeves".
- Some writers might want to rearrange words and rework lines to make their poems rhyme.

Showing Off

- After the students have recopied their poems, ask each student to choose his or her strongest line.
- Let each student add his or her strongest line to a collaborative poem by writing the line on a long strip of paper with a marker.
- When everyone has written a line, the group should decide on a title for the poem.
- Hang the poem from a hanger or wooden dowel in a place where everyone can enjoy their creation. (See page 111.)

Don't You Just Hate. . . .

...when someone scrapes a fingernail across the chalkboard?

...when you go to the freezer for ice and the tray is empty because someone forgot to refill it?

...when your mother blames you for something your brother or sister did?

...when you trip over your own feet in front of a lot of people?

...when somebody borrows your bike without asking?

...when the toothpaste tube is mashed in the middle?

Add more of your own.

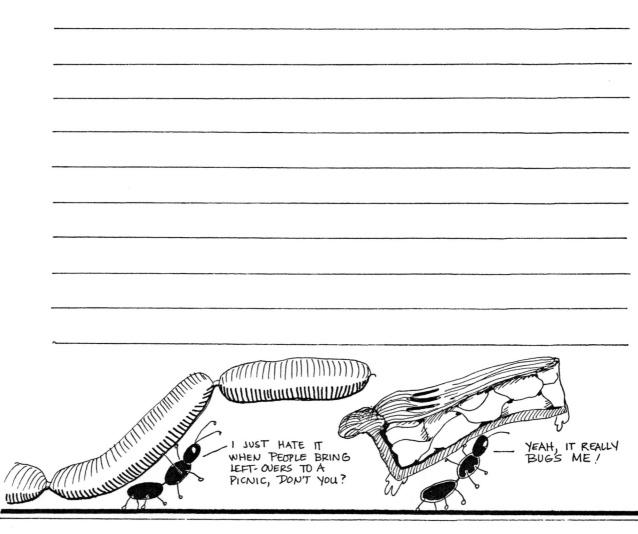

I JUST HATE IT WHEN PEOPLE BRING LEFT-OVERS TO A PICNIC, DON'T YOU?

YEAH, IT REALLY BUGS ME!

I HATE IT WHEN...

I GET BLAMED FOR SOMETHING I DIDNT DO.

it rains on my birthday.

I have to eat the school lunch.

MY mother uses MY bike.

nobody ever knocks before coming into my room.

MY BROTHER KEEPS CHANGING CHANNELS.

bubble gum gets in my hair.

we have to go to school during a big snowstorm.

SOMEONE CUTS IN FRONT OF ME IN LINE.

my little sister gets in my closet.

we have asparagus again.

People crack their knuckles.

my best friend decides to play with somebody else.

recess is cancelled.

we have to clean our desks out.

I get something stuck between my teeth.

I STUDY HARD for A TEST AND MISS A LOT OF PROBLEMS. Summer ends.

A TACO BREAKS APART ON THE 1st BITE.

Somebody pulls my hair!

I get a paper cut.

people tease me about my freckles.

Examples

27. A Ticklish Matter

feather

plummeting

flying

springy

floating

dandelion

dizzy

escaping

light

Materials
- small feathers (Hackle feathers are available at craft and hobby stores.)
- writing paper and pencils
- construction paper
- hole punch
- glue
- string

Romancing
- Have each student stand with a partner in a place where there is room to move around. Agree on a signal for getting quiet to listen. Give these directions to the students, one at a time, stopping after each direction to quiet the group.

1) Blow your feather high into the air. Your partner should try to catch the feather before it hits the ground.
2) Now you try to catch the feather on your head.
3) Take turns trying to catch the feather with your knee...hip...elbow...back...shoulder...toe...etc.

OOPS!

fluff

tickler

swaying

tossing

down

Collecting
1) Give each pair of partners a copy of the student page "Fantastic, Floating, Flipping Feathers" (page 114), on which they may write words, phrases, and ideas about feathers. (Continue to direct each step.)
2) Instruct the students to list adjectives that describe the look, feel, and color of their feathers. (Label this list 1.)
3) Have the students list participles (ing verbs) that describe the actions and movements of their feathers. (Label this list 2.)

4) Have the students finish the following similes in several different ways.

My feather is as fluffy as _____ .
My feather is as light as _____ .
My feather is as soft as _____ .

Note: Students may write two or more endings for each simile. Students should write the similes on a sheet of paper. (Label this list 3.)

5) Instruct the students to list synonyms for the word "feather" (example: plume). (Students should label this list 4.)

Writing

- Direct the students as follows.
  Line 1 Write the word "feather".
  Line 2 Choose two favorite words from list 1. (adjectives) Write the words next to each other with a comma between them.
  Line 3 Choose three favorite words from list 2. (participles) Write the words next to each other with commas between them.
  Line 4 Choose one simile ending from list 3 to fill in the following blanks.
  fluffy as _____ , light as _____ , soft as _____
  Line 5 Choose one synonym for feather from list 4.

Praising

- Comment on combinations of words that "flow" together. (twisting, twirling, tumbling)
- Point out unique word choices and unusual similes.

Polishing

- Ask the students to review their lines by answering these questions:
  Lines 2 & 3 Have you chosen words that are interesting and that sound good together? Do you like the order of the words? Would the words sound better rearranged?
  Line 4 Could you have chosen a more unusual simile?
  Line 5 Does your word choice make a good ending? (You may use the word "feather" for line 5 if no other word suits your poem.)

Showing Off

- Have the students recopy their final poems on white paper.
- Students may make feather "creatures" and glue them around their poems for decoration.

soft

light

feather

twirly

silken

dizzy

smooth

elusive

tossing

wild

angry

Fantastic, Floating, Flipping Feathers

List 1

List 2

List 3

List 4

Line 1 _____

Line 2 _____

Line 3 _____

Line 4 _____

Line 5 _____

feather
crazy, dizzy
swishing, swaying, staggering
soft as dandelion fluff
down

FEATHER
TRICKY, TWIRLY
TWISTING, TOSSING, TUMBLING
LIGHT AS A TEARDROP
TICKLER

feather
purple, unpredictable
wiggling, wobbling, plummeting
wild as an angry bumblebee
plume

feather
silken, smooth
sinking, escaping, disappearing
elusive as a spring butterfly
fluff

Examples

28. Me . . . Now And Then

I JUST LOVE LOOKING THROUGH THE FAMILY ALBUM

Materials

- writing paper and pencils
- photograph of each student at a younger age (about age five)
- small mirrors (or very recent photographs)
- thick, black markers
- crayons or small markers
- large drawing paper
- colored construction paper

Romancing

- Have the students look at the photographs of themselves when they were younger and then look in the mirrors (or at their recent photographs).
- Ask the students to talk about what they used to be like and how they're different now.
- Let the students take turns telling stories about their childhoods.

Collecting

- Ask the students to think and talk about the following specifics, making comparisons to the present.

  how you looked
  what you did with your time
  what you liked/didn't like
  what you were afraid of
  what you're afraid of now
  what you thought or believed
  what you couldn't do then that you can do now
  what you got into trouble for doing

- Have the students add their own ideas to the list above.

the name design "Mary"

mounted "Me Poem"

Writing

1) Give each student a copy of the "Me-Stuff" student page (page 118).
2) Direct the students to complete the first pair of sentences in regard to their personal appearances.

   I used to _____ .
   But now I _____ .

3) Guide the students through one pair of sentences at a time. Instruct the students to complete the sentences by following directions such as:

   describe something you used to do and something you do now
   describe something you used to fear and something you fear now
   describe what used to anger you and what angers you now

   Note: The students will need to adapt the form: I used to be, I may become, I used to like...think...believe...have...wish, etc.

4) Allow the students to complete a few pairs on their own.

Praising

- Instruct the students to share their sentences with each other and to look for interesting, amusing, or surprising ideas.

Polishing

- Ask the students to be sure they haven't left out anything interesting about themselves.
- Remind the students to check the order of the lines. Each student should choose a good opening and closing sentence.
- Each student should choose a good title.

Showing Off

- Have the students make name designs by drawing the letters of their first names in various positions on large pieces of drawing paper (see page 116). Tell the students to use wide, black markers.
- Instruct the students to fill in the spaces between the lines with interesting color designs using crayons or markers.
- Have the students copy their poems on clean paper. Students may glue colored construction paper to the backs of their poems and mount the poems on top of their name designs. Have the students mount their name designs on colored construction paper. They also might like to glue photos to the fronts of their designs.

117

Me-Stuff

_____ (Title)

I used to _____ ,

but now I _____ .

I used to _____ ,

but now I _____ .

I used to _____ ,

but now I _____ .

I used to _____ ,

but now I _____ .

I used to _____ ,

but now I _____ .

I used to _____ ,

but now I _____ .

I used to _____ ,

but now I _____ .

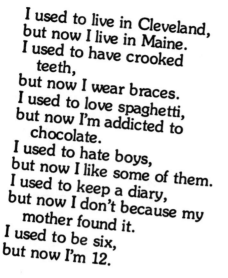

I used to live in Cleveland,
but now I live in Maine.
I used to have crooked
    teeth,
but now I wear braces.
I used to love spaghetti,
but now I'm addicted to
    chocolate.
I used to hate boys,
but now I like some of them.
I used to keep a diary,
but now I don't because my
    mother found it.
I used to be six,
but now I'm 12.

I used to have a chubby face,
but now it is scrawny.
I used to be clumsy,
but now I'm coordinated.
I used to hate vegetables,
but now I hate homework.
I used to think my dad knew
    everything,
but now I know better.
I used to be afraid of
    monsters,
but now I'm afraid of strangers.
I used to wish for new toys,
but now I wish for athletic
    skill.
I used to want to be 10,
but now I can't wait to be 16.

Examples

29. So Sorry!

Materials
- paper
- construction paper, fabric pieces, or poster board
- pencils
- scissors
- glue

Romancing
- Read aloud "This Is Just To Say", a poem by William Carlos Williams found in REFLECTIONS ON A GIFT OF WATERMELON PICKLE and other poetry collections. (Or, you may choose to read the apology poem below.)
- Read the apologies on page 123 to the class.

Collecting
- Ask students to tell the class about times they've apologized for doing something for which they were not really sorry.
- Make a list on the chalkboard of things the students have apologized for doing that they were not truly sorry they had done.

Writing
1) Have the class select a topic to work on together. Help the students use their own ideas to write a class apology poem, following the form below:

What I did	I just hit a softball through the dining room window,
Why I'm not happy about it	And I know you're having company for dinner.
Ask to be Forgiven	Forgive me.
Why I'm not truly sorry	But it was a fine hit, and I made a home run.

2) Give each student a copy of the student page "My Apology" (page 122), and let each student follow the form to write an apology poem.

Note: Students need not follow the form exactly. Each part of the poem may have any number of lines.

Praising

- Point out interesting, brief beginnings that clearly state a misdeed.
- Look for strong words that make the apology sound convincing.
- Point out phrases that make the rewards of doing the deed seem to outweigh the possible punishment (ie: "a fine hit").

Polishing

- The students should check to see that the four parts of the form have been included.
- Have the students give their poems interesting titles.
- Have the students add or substitute words to improve unconvincing apologies.
- Each student should rework the last section, if necessary, to make it clear that he or she is not really sorry.

Showing Off

- The students can make "I'm sorry" banners, pennants, flags, kites, or windsocks on which to "fly" their poems. (See the illustrated instructions below for making windsocks.)

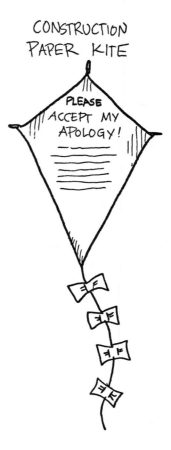

CONSTRUCTION PAPER KITE

PLEASE ACCEPT MY APOLOGY!

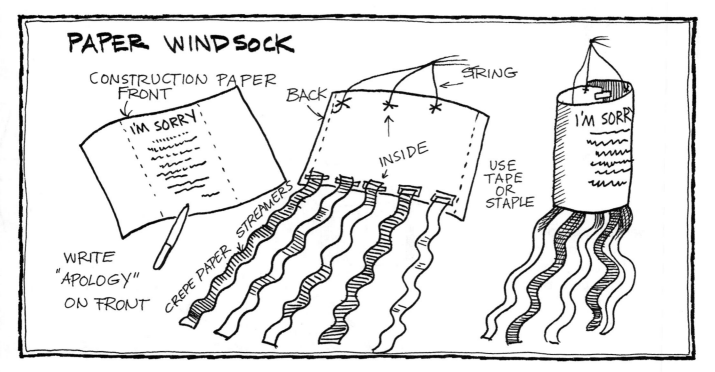

PAPER WINDSOCK

CONSTRUCTION PAPER FRONT

I'M SORRY

BACK

STRING

INSIDE

USE TAPE OR STAPLE

CREPE PAPER STREAMERS

WRITE "APOLOGY" ON FRONT

I'M SORRY

My Apology

Write an apology poem for something you've done or might have done that was not a good idea, but that you weren't really sorry for doing.

_____ (Title)

What you did

_____

_____

_____

Why someone is likely to be unhappy about it

_____

_____

_____

Your apology or request for forgiveness

_____

_____

_____

Why you did it and why you're not really sorry

_____

_____

Don't forget to give your poem a title. Show off your poem by making an "I'm sorry" banner or a special frame for your poem.

Dear Mikki,
I broke your best new kite before you even had a chance to fly it. I'm so sorry, but I've never seen a kite fly so high!
Love, Lester

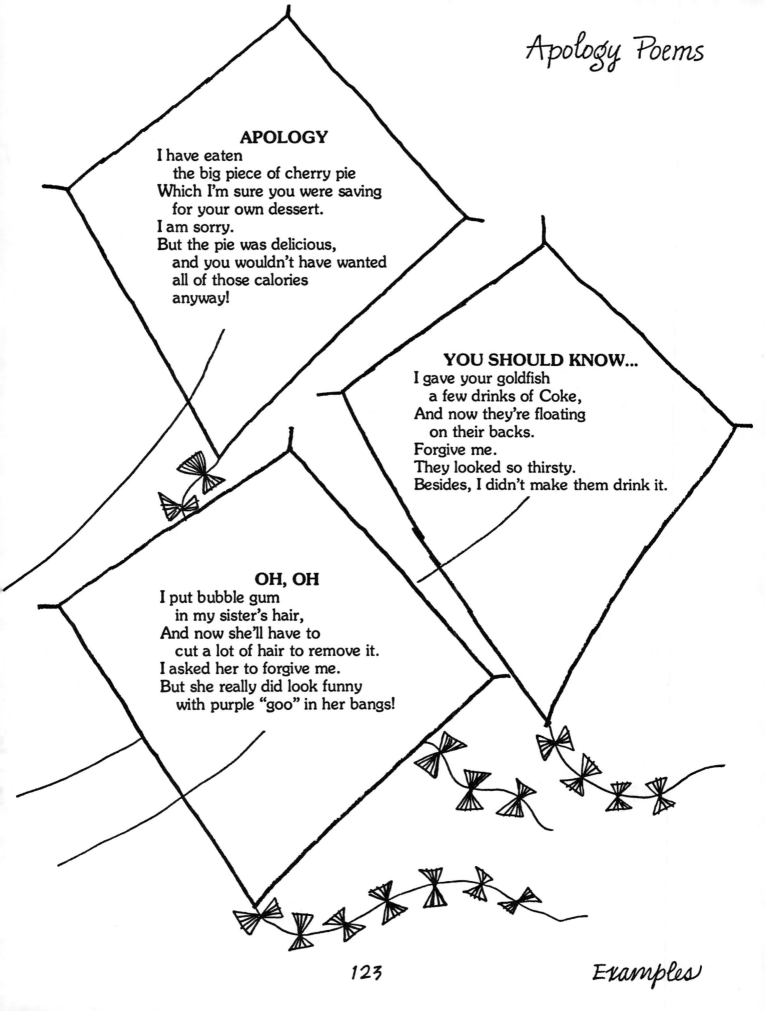

APOLOGY

I have eaten
   the big piece of cherry pie
Which I'm sure you were saving
   for your own dessert.
I am sorry.
But the pie was delicious,
   and you wouldn't have wanted
   all of those calories
   anyway!

YOU SHOULD KNOW...

I gave your goldfish
   a few drinks of Coke,
And now they're floating
   on their backs.
Forgive me.
They looked so thirsty.
Besides, I didn't make them drink it.

OH, OH

I put bubble gum
   in my sister's hair,
And now she'll have to
   cut a lot of hair to remove it.
I asked her to forgive me.
But she really did look funny
   with purple "goo" in her bangs!

Examples

30. The Surf's Up

*"Painted" Poetry
Ideas:*

*Tornado
Peacock
Octopus
Rainbow
Sunset
Parachute
Pesty Fly
Falling Leaf
Mountain Climbing
Rollercoaster
Going Down-
Stairs*

Materials
- colored chalk
- large, white drawing paper
- mural paper
- spray fixative
- newspaper
- colored construction paper

Romancing
- Share with the class one or more examples of "painted writing" which are written on poster board or the chalkboard. Use samples from page 127 or create your own.
- Discuss how the shape of the writing "expresses" what the writing is about.
- Explain that "painted writing" is a way of placing words on paper to give a visual effect to match the "feeling" of the writing.
- Have the class brainstorm to write a list of other topics that would be good for "painted writings".

Collecting
- Ask the students to use copies of the student page "Once Upon A Wave" (page 126) as a guide to collect ideas for a group "painted poem" about a wave or the ocean.
- Write the collected words, phrases, and ideas on the board as the students write them on paper.

Writing
1) Ask questions to help the students combine words and phrases into lines for the poem.
2) Build several good lines as a class.

Praising
- Look for strong words that describe the motion, sound, smell, or appearance of water, the ocean, or waves.
- Point out lines and phrases that are appealing to the senses.
- Look for good uses of imagery and striking metaphors.

124

Polishing
- Instruct the students to eliminate any lines that are too much alike.
- Help the class choose good beginning and ending lines. Have the students arrange the other lines in an order that "flows".
- The class should try to add at least two more vivid words to the poem.

Showing Off
- Copy the finished poem in large letters on a piece of mural paper. Let the students help decide how to place the words on the paper so as to give a strong visual "feel" for the topic.
- Have a couple of students strengthen the visual idea by adding color to the words with strokes of colored chalk or crayon.

More Painted Writing
- Let the students choose their own topics for individual poems.
- Make sure the students write the words large enough to fill most of the paper. The students should add the chalk design after they have finished writing their poems. Remind the students that the goal is to make the words "paint" the picture.
- Spray the poems (outdoors) with fixative so the chalk won't smear. (Laminate the poems if possible.) The students may frame or mount their "painted poems" on colored construction paper.

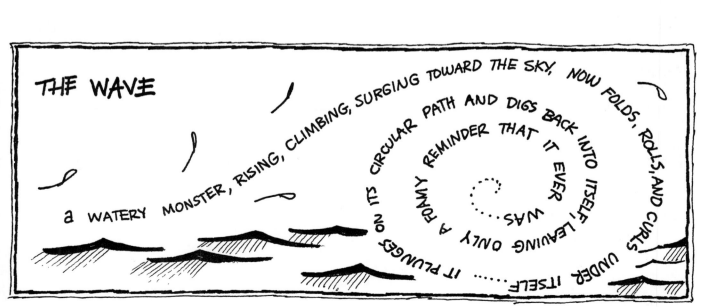

THE WAVE

a watery monster, rising, climbing, surging toward the sky, now folds, rolls, and curls under itself...... it plunges on its circular path and digs back into itself, leaving only a foamy reminder that it ever was...

Once Upon A Wave

How does a wave look? (Write descriptive words and phrases.)

How do waves sound?

How does sea air smell and taste?

What sensations do you feel when standing on a beach near a pounding surf?

Think about being caught in a large wave. What is the wave doing? (Write action words.)

Finish each sentence below in one or more ways.

A wave is like ——————————————————————————— .

The surf sounds like ——————————————————————— .

Waves make me think of ——————————————————————— .

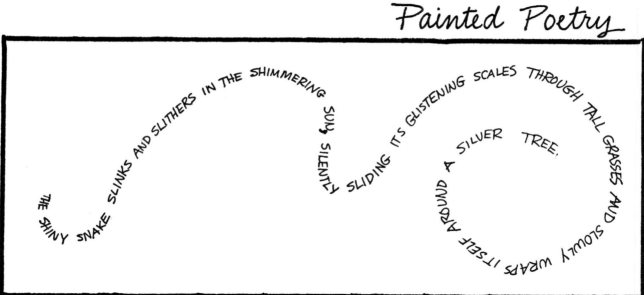

THE SHINY SNAKE SLINKS AND SLITHERS IN THE SHIMMERING SUN, SILENTLY SLIDING ITS GLISTENING SCALES THROUGH TALL GRASSES AND SLOWLY WRAPS ITSELF AROUND A SILVER TREE.

THE HAPPY BOUNCING BALL CAME dancing AND playing AND hopping UP AND DOWN THE STREET.

FLAPPING, FLOATING, SWEEPING, SOARING, SLEEK AND SOFT, THE FEATHERY FLOCK GENTLY BEATS ITS SILVERED WINGS IN SMOOTH RYTHM....WITH HARDLY A SOUND.

PoExamples